HARVEY

HARVEY

by Mary Chase

JOSEF WEINBERGER PLAYS

LONDON

First published in the United Kingdom in 1952 by
Josef Weinberger Ltd
(pka English Theatre Guild Ltd)
12-14 Mortimer Street, London, W1T 3JJ

ISBN 0 85676 137 0

Printed by Commercial Colour Press Plc, Hainault, Essex IG6 3HX.

HARVEY was produced by Brock Pemberton at the Forty-Eighth Street Theatre, New York City, on November 1 1944. It was directed by Antoinette Perry, with settings by John Root. The cast was as follows:

MYRTLE MAE SIMMONS	Jane Van Duser
VETA LOUISE SIMMONS	Josephine Hull
ELWOOD P DOWD	Frank Fay
MISS JOHNSON	Eloise Sheldon
MRS ETHEL CHAUVENET	Frederica Going
RUTH KELLY, RN	Janet Tyler
DUANE WILSON	Jesse White
LYMAN SANDERSON, MD	Tom Seidel
WILLIAM R CHUMLEY, MD	Fred Irving Lewis
BETTY CHUMLEY	Dora Clement
JUDGE OMAR GAFFNEY	John Kirk
E J LOFGREN	Robert Gist

HARVEY was first presented in the United Kingdom by Val Parnell in conjunction with George and Alfred Black and HM Tennent Ltd, in association with Brock Pemberton, at the Prince of Wales Theatre, London on January 5 1949. It was directed by Anthony Quale and the cast was as follows:

MYRTLE MAE SIMMONS	Rosaline Haddon
VETA LOUISE SIMMONS	Athene Seyler
ELWOOD P DOWD	Sid Field
MISS JOHNSON	Henzie Raeburn
MRS ETHEL CHAUVENET	Violet Farebrother
RUTH KELLY, RN	Diana Fawcett
MARVIN WILSON	Henry Gilbert
LYMAN SANDERSON, MD	Jeremy Hawk
WILLIAM R CHUMLEY, MD	Ernest Hare
BETTY CHUMLEY	Margery Caldicott
JUDGE OMAR GAFFNEY	Gordon Phillott
E J LOFGREN	Harry Herbert

SCENE SYNOPSIS

The action of the play takes place in a city in the Far West in the library of the old Dowd family mansion, and the reception room of Chumley's Rest.

Time: The Present

ACT ONE

Scene One:	The Library, late afternoon.
Scene Two:	Chumley's Rest, an hour later.

ACT TWO

Scene One:	The Library, an hour later.
Scene Two:	Chumley's Rest, four hours later.

ACT THREE

Chumley's Rest, a few minutes later.

ACT ONE

SCENE 1

TIME: *Late afternoon of a spring day. The present.*

SET: *The library of the old Dowd family mansion – a room lined with books and set with heavy, old-fashioned furniture of a faded grandeur. The most conspicuous item in the room is an oil painting over a black marble Victorian mantelpiece at the lower part of the wall at stage* L. *This is the portrait of a lantern-jawed older woman. There are double doors, open, at* R., *leading to the hallway and parlour, which is not seen. There is a single door at* U.S.L.C., *closed. There are bookcases* L. *and* R., *and in front of bookcase* L. *there is a table on which stands some flowers, a telephone and a tray of drinks. There is a round table,* R., *with a bowl of flowers on it, and arm-chairs* L. *and* R. *of table. From off-stage,* R., *comes the sound of a female voice singing "Pale hands I love."*

AT RISE: *The stage is empty. the telephone begins to ring.* MYRTLE MAE SIMMONS *runs on from* R. *She goes to the telephone and answers it.*

MYRTLE	(*To phone*) Mrs Simmons? Well, Mrs Simmons is my mother, but she has guests this afternoon. Who wants her? (*Respectful change in voice.*) Oh, wait just a minute...hang on just a minute. (*Lays receiver on table and goes to doorway,* R., *calling off.*) Mother! (*Beckons insistently.*) Mother!
VETA	(*Entering* R.) Yes, dear?
MYRTLE	Telephone.
VETA	(*Turning to go out again*) Oh no, dear. Not with all of them in there. Say I'm busy.
MYRTLE	But, mother it's the Society Editor – of the *Eldorado Evening News*....

VETA
(*Turning*) Oh, the Society Editor. She's very important. (*She goes to the phone, fixes her hair and assumes dignified pose.*) Good afternoon, Miss Ellerbe. This is Veta Simmons. Yes – a tea and reception for the members of the Women's Higher Discussion Group; in honour of its founder; my mother, you know, the late Marcella Pinny Dowd. (*Extravagant gesture to picture.*)

(MYRTLE *is watching out of door* R.)

Myrtle! – how many would you say?

MYRTLE
Oh, seventy-five at least.

VETA
(*On phone*) Seventy-five! Miss Tewkesbury is the soloist, accompanied by Miss Wilda McCurdy, accompanist.

MYRTLE
Come on, mother, Miss Tewkesbury is almost finished with her number.

VETA
She'll do an encore.

MYRTLE
Well, what if they don't give her a lot of applause?

VETA
I've known her for years. She'll do an encore. Miss Ellerbe, you might say that I am entertaining assisted by my daughter, Miss Myrtle Mae Simmons. (*To* MYRTLE, *indicating her dress.*) Myrtle, what colour would you call that?

MYRTLE
(*Crossing to* C.) Oh, Rancho Rose, so they told me.

VETA
(*On phone*) Miss Myrtle Mae Simmons looks charming in a Rancho Rose toned crêpe, picked out of the girdle with a touch of magenta on emerald. I wish you could see her, Miss Ellerbe.

MYRTLE	(*Crossing back to doorway,* R.) Mother, please – she's almost finished. And where's the waitress?
VETA	Everything's ready. The moment she's finished singing we open the dining-room doors and begin pouring. ("*Pouring*" *gesture with free hand. Into phone.*) Yes, Miss Ellerbe, this is the first party we've had in years. There's a reason – but I don't want it in the papers. We all have our troubles, Miss Ellerbe. The guest list?
MYRTLE	Mother, come!
	(*The singing off-stage finishes, and applause is heard.*)
Veta	Well, if you'll excuse me now, Miss Ellerbe, I'll find the guest list and call you later. (*Hangs up.*)
MYRTLE	(*Crossing to* C.) Mother! – Mrs Chauvenet's just come in.
VETA	Mrs Chauvenet! Now, Myrtle, you must be very nice to Mrs Chauvenet – she has a grandson about your age.
MYRTLE	Oh, mother, I only hope Uncle Elwood doesn't come in.
VETA	Now, Myrtle, remember! We agreed not to talk about that this afternoon. The whole point of this party is to get you started. We work through those older women to the younger group.
MYRTLE	The only reason we can have a party this afternoon is because Uncle Elwood is tied up with his friends playing poker. Thank heavens for poker! We can't have anyone here in the evenings, and that's when men come to see you – (*Sits on arm of chair,* R.C.) in the evenings.

VETA   (*At* C.) I know, darling; but they'll have to invite you out. It won't hurt them one bit. Oh, Myrtle, you've got so much to offer! Well, I don't care what anyone says – there's something sweet about every young girl, and a man takes that sweetness, and look what he does with it. But you've got to meet somebody, Myrtle, that's all there is to it.

MYRTLE   And if I do, they'll say, "That's Myrtle Mae Simmons. Her uncle is Elwood P. Dowd – the biggest screwball in the town. Elwood P. Dowd and his pal ..."

VETA   (*Stopping her with a gesture*) Now! you promised.

MYRTLE   I'm sorry, mother. Oh, let's get them into the dining-room. (*Rise and crosses below table to doorway,* D.R.)

VETA   (*At* C.) Now when the members come in here and you make your little speech to welcome on behalf of your grandmother, be sure to do this...(*Makes extravagant gesture towards picture over mantelpiece.*)

MYRTLE   (*Standing in doorway, facing* VETA. *In disgust*) And then after that I mention my Uncle Elwood and say a few words about his pal Harvey!

VETA   Myrtle!

MYRTLE   Damn Harvey!

     (VETA *runs over to* MYRTLE *and pushes her* D.S.)

VETA   Myrtle! That's right – let everybody hear you! (*She closes the doors.*) You said that name! You promised you wouldn't say that name, and you said it.

MYRTLE   I'm sorry, mother, but how do you know Uncle Elwood won't come in and introduce Harvey to everybody?

VETA	(*Crossing above table to* L.C.) This is unkind of you, Myrtle. Elwood is the biggest headache I have. Even if people do call him peculiar, he's still my brother. But he won't be home this afternoon.
MYRTLE	Are you sure?
VETA	Of course I'm sure. (*She gives a sudden start and looks over her shoulder towards the door,* L.C.)
MYRTLE	(*Sitting chair* R.C.) Oh, mother, why can't we live like other people?
VETA	Must I remind you again? Elwood is not living with us – we are living with him.
MYRTLE	Living with him and Harvey! (*Points to picture.*) Did grandmother know about Harvey?
VETA	I've wondered and wondered about that. But she never wrote me if she did.
MYRTLE	Why did she leave all her property to Uncle Elwood?
VETA	Well, I suppose it was because she died in his arms. People are sentimental about things like that.
MYRTLE	You always say that, and it doesn't make sense. She couldn't make out her will after she died, could she?
VETA	(*Crossing to doors,* D.R.) Don't be didactic, Myrtle Mae. It's not becoming in a young girl, and men loathe it.
	(*She opens the doors, and the sound of talking and rattling of teacups is heard off-stage.*)
VETA	Now, don't forget.
	(*Gestures to picture of Marcella and exits.* MYRTLE *goes to doorway, gestures half-heartedly to picture and exits, closing the doors behind her. Through door* L.C. *enters* ELWOOD P. DOWD. *He is a man about forty-seven years old, with*

a dignified bearing and yet a dreamy expression in his eyes. His expression is benign yet serious to the point of gravity. He wears a Trilby hat with the brim turned up. Over his arm he carries another hat and coat. He ushers in an invisible person, bows him over to chair, R.C., then places the second hat and coat on the table.)

ELWOOD Come in, Harvey. Come on in. That's right. Now there's your hat and there's your coat. Now then, sit down – make yourself at home.

(The telephone rings.)

Oh, excuse me, Harvey. *(Crosses L.C.)* Are you all right there? *(Picks up phone. Into phone.)* Hallo. Oh, you've got the wrong number – but how are you anyhow? This is Elwood P. Dowd speaking. I'll do? Well thank you very much. And what is your name, my dear? Miss Elsie Porringer; oh, Bollinger. Harvey *(to chair R.C.)*, this is a Miss Elsie Bollinger. *(To phone.)* And how are you today, Miss Bollinger? That's fine. Yes, my dear I should be happy to join your club. I belong to several clubs already – the University Club, the Country Club, the poker club down at the Police Headquarters; I spend a good deal of my time down there and at Charlie's Place, and over at Eddie's Bar. And what is your club, my dear? *(He attempts to speak several times, but the person at the other end will not let him get a word in. He makes gestures of despair towards the chair, R.C.)* Really; hang on a minute. *(To chair.)* Harvey, I can get the *Ladies Home Journal, Good Housekeeping and The Open Road for Boys* for two years for six dollars twenty-five. *(To phone.)* That sounds pretty good to me, Miss Bollinger; I'll join that. *(To phone.)* Harvey says it sounds pretty good to him too. Yes. That will be two subscriptions, and mail everything to this address. I hope to have the pleasure of

meeting you some time, Miss Bollinger.
Really? Hold on a minute. (*To chair.*) Harvey,
she says she'd like to meet me. (*To phone.*)
When? When would you like to meet me?
Well, why not right now? It seems my sister is
having some friends in, and we'd be very
happy if you'd come over and join us. Not at
all – my sister will be delighted. 343, Temple
Drive. We'll expect you in a few minutes.
Good-bye for now, Miss Bollinger. (*He raises
his hat and hangs up the phone. To chair.*) Well,
Harvey, she's coming over. Well, don't you
think we ought to freshen up a little? Yes –
so do I. Well, come on, old soul. (*He picks up
the hat and coat from table,* R., *and motions the
invisible person towards the door.*) Oh, after you,
No, no, after you. Well, my dear fellow, you
are a guest in my house. That's right –
straight down the corridor – just at the end.

(*Exits door* L.C. VETA *enters* D.R. *followed by*
MAID.)

VETA   I can't seem to remember where I put that
                guest list. I must read it to Miss Ellerbe. Have
                you seen it, Johnson?

MAID   (*Looking under cushions on chair,* R.C.) No, Mrs
                Simmons.

VETA   Well, look on my dressing-table.

MAID   Yes, Mrs Simmons.

                (MAID *exits* L.C. MYRTLE *enters* D.R.)

MYRTLE   Mother – here's Mrs Chauvenet – she's
                asking for you. (*Turning, speaking to someone in
                the hall.*) Here's Mother, Mrs Chauvenet.

(*Enter* MRS CHAUVENET, D.R. *She is a woman of sixty-five or sixty-eight, a heavy dresser with the casual sumptuousness of a wealthy Western woman – in silvery gold and plush, with mink scarf, even though it is a spring day. She rushes over to* VETA.)

MRS. C.   Ah – Veta Louise Simmons!

VETA   (*Meeting her,* C.) Aunt Ethel!

MRS. C.   (*Kissing her*) I thought you were dead.

VETA   (*Motioning to* MYRTLE *to come forward and meet the great lady*) Oh no, I'm very much alive, thank you. ...

MRS. C.   (*Turning to Myrtle at* R.C.) And this full-grown girl is your daughter. I've known you since you were a baby.

MYRTLE   I know.

MRS. C.   What's your name, dear?

VETA   (*Proudly*) This is Myrtle, Aunt Ethel. Myrtle Mae. ...

MRS. C.   MYRTLE Mae! Why, you're your grandmother all over again. I was at her funeral. Now, where's Elwood?

VETA   (*With a nervous glance at* MYRTLE MAE) Elwood coudn't be here this afternoon, Aunt Ethel. Now, let me get you some tea.

            (*She takes* MRS CHAUVENET *by the hand and crosses with her below table towards doorway* D.R.)

MRS. C.   But shame on him. That was the main reason I came. I want to see Elwood. (*She turns obstinately away.*)

VETA   Now come along, there are lots of people anxious to talk to you.

MRS. C.   (*Sitting chair* L. *of table*) Do you realise that it's years since I've seen Elwood?

MRS. C.	Simply years. I was saying to Mr Chauvenet only the other evening, "What on earth do you suppose has happened to Elwood Dowd? He never comes to the Club dances any more, and I haven't seen him at a horse show for years." (*Turning to* VETA.) Does Elwood see anybody nowadays, Veta Louise?
VETA	(*Glancing at* MYRTLE) Oh yes, Aunt Ethel. Elwood sees somebody.
MYRTLE	Oh, yes.
MRS. C.	(*To* MYRTLE) Your Uncle Elwood is one of my favourite people.
VETA	I remember.
MRS. C.	Always has been. Now, is Elwood happy, Veta Louise?
VETA	Elwood's very happy, Aunt Ethel. You don't need to worry about Elwood. (*Moves to* U.S. *of table and looks out through doorway,* D.R.) Why, there's Mrs Frank Cummings just come in. Don't you want to meet her?
MRS. C.	Mrs Frank Cummings! (*She chuckles delightedly and crosses above chair to* L. *of* VETA *to peer out through doorway.*) My, but she looks ghastly! Hasn't she failed, though?
VETA	If you think *she* looks badly, wait till you see him!
MRS. C.	Is that so? I must ask him over. (*Looks again.*) She looks frightful. (*To* MYRTLE.) You know, I thought she was dead. Now what about that tea, Veta? (*Turns to chair to pick up her scarf.*)
VETA	Why, certainly, Aunt Ethel. ...
	(VETA *starts to lead the way through the doorway* D.R. ELWOOD *enters* U.L. MRS CHAUVENET *sees him as she picks up her scarf; she rushes towards him.*)

MRS. C.   Elwood Dowd! Bless your heart!

ELWOOD   Aunt Ethel! What a pleasure to come in and find a beautiful lady waiting for me! (*They embrace.*)

MRS. C.   Elwood, you haven't changed. (*She waggles her finger at him.*)

(VETA *and* MYRTLE *rushes forward to* MRS. CHAUVENET *and try to push her out of the room,* D.R.)

VETA   Now come along, Aunt Ethel; you mustn't miss the party.

MYRTLE   There's punch if you don't like tea.

MRS. C.   (*Breaking away and returning to* ELWOOD) But I do like tea. Now stop pulling at me you two. Elwood, what night next week can you come to dinner?

ELWOOD   Any night. Any night at all, Aunt Ethel. I'd be delighted.

VETA   (*Moves* D.S *to* R. *of table, followed by* MYRTLE) Elwood, there's some mail for you today! I took it up to your room. (*She waves to* ELWOOD *to leave.*)

ELWOOD   (*Waving back*) Oh, thank you, Veta. That was nice of you. And now, Aunt Ethel, I must introduce you to Harvey.

(VETA *and* MYRTLE *turn away in despair,* VETA *standing by chair* R. *of table,* MYRTLE *against* D.S. *side of doorway.* ELWOOD *turns towards chair beside him.*)

Harvey, you've heard me speak to Mrs
Chauvenet – we always call her Aunt Ethel.
One of my oldest and dearest friends. (*Nods
as though having heard someone beside him speak.*)
Yes, that's right. This is the one. Yes – she's
the one. (*To* MRS CHAUVENET.) Oh Aunt
Ethel, Harvey says he would have known you
anywhere.

(MRS CHAUVENET *has been looking bewildered,
craning her neck to see behind* ELWOOD. *He bows
to her, and as she bows back, with a forced laugh,
he crosses* D.S. *of her towards* VETA *and* MYRTLE
to above table, R.C.)

Why, Veta and Myrtle, you both look lovely.
(*To Air.*) Now, Harvey, don't you think we'd
better say hullo to all our friends? Yes? Come
on, then. (*To* MRS CHAUVENET.) Oh, Aunt
Ethel, please...

MRS. C.   What?

ELWOOD   Well, my dear, you're rather standing in his
way!

(*She moves up stage to let the invisible* HARVEY
pass.)

ELWOOD   That's right. (*To* HARVEY.) Now then, let's get
you fixed up for the party. (*He pantomimes
fixing* HARVEY'S *tie and arranging his hair and
ears.*) That's better. Now go right on in – I'll
be with you in a minute. (*He ushers him out,*
D.R., *then turns back to* MRS CHAUVENET *to find
her staring at him in horror.*) Oh, Aunt Ethel,
you seem a little disturbed about Harvey.

MRS. C.   Yes, well...

ELWOOD   Oh, please don't be. He stares like that at
everybody. It's just his way. But he liked
you, I could tell; he liked you very much.
(*Crossing to doorway,* D.R., *he speaks to* HARVEY,
off-stage, as he makes his exit.) Oh, Harvey, let
me introduce you to a Mrs. ...

(*After* ELWOOD'S *exit all are silent. Finally* VETA *clears her throat, echoed severely by* MRS CHAUVENET.)

VETA

(*Beginning to cross to* MRS CHAUVENET *below table,* R.) Some tea perhaps?

MRS. C.

Well...I think not just now; I'll be running along. (*She gathers up her bag and gloves from the table.*) But I'll be talking to you quite soon – goodbye. Goodbye. (*And as she exits through door,* L.C.) Well! Elwood Dowd! Of all that...

(MYRTLE *rushes to* U.S. *of doorway,* D.R., *looking out.*)

MYRTLE

Oh! He's introducing Harvey to everybody. Oh lord! (*Runs towards door,* L.C.)

VETA

Myrtle! Where are you going?

MYRTLE

Up to my room. I can't face those people now. Oh, I wish I was dead.

VETA

(*Crosses to* MYRTLE, *pulling her back from door*) Come back here. Stay with me. We'll get him out of there and upstairs to his own room.

MYRTLE

Oh no, mother, I can't.

VETA

Now ... pretend I'm fixing your girdle.

(VETA *fiddles with* MYRTLE'S *girdle. They are in line with the two doorways,* VETA *facing* L., MYRTLE R.)

MYRTLE

Oh, mother!

VETA

Now pretend we're having a gay little chat. Keep looking, and when you catch his eye tell me. He always comes when I call him. Now then, do you see him yet?

MYRTLE

(*In tears*) No – not yet. How do you do Mrs Cummings?

VETA	Smile, can't you! Have you no pride? (*Looks off* R. *and gives an obvious false smile.*) I'm smiling, and he's my own brother.
MYRTLE	Oh, mother – people get run over by lorries every day. Why can't something like that happen to Uncle Elwood?
VETA	Myrtle Mae Simmons, I'm ashamed of you! This thing is not your Uncle Elwood's fault.
	(*The telephone rings.*)
	Ah! That'll be Miss Ellerbe. Now keep looking, keep smiling. (*She goes to the phone.*)
MYRTLE	Mrs Cummings is leaving now. Uncle Elwood must have told her what Harvey is.
VETA	(*To phone*) Hullo. This is Mrs Simmons. Should you come in the clothes you have on? Well, what have you on? Who is this? Miss Bollinger? But I don't know any Miss Bollinger. Should you what? May I inquire who invited you? Mr Dowd! Well, thank you very much, but I think there's been a mistake. (*Rings off. To* MYRTLE.) Well I never!
MYRTLE	Never what?
VETA	One of your Uncle Elwood's friends. She asked me if she should bring a quart of gin to the party.
MYRTLE	(*Looking out and pointing off*) There he is – he's talking to Mrs Reynolds.
VETA	Is Harvey with him? (*She crosses* MYRTLE *towards doorway* D.R.)
MYRTLE	(*At* C.) Well, what a thing to ask! How can I tell?
VETA	(*Calling through doorway*) Oh, Elwood!
ELWOOD	(*Off*) Yes, dear.
VETA	Could I speak to you a minute?

VETA   (*Turning back to* MYRTLE) Now, I promise
                you your uncle has disgraced us for the last
                time in this house. I'm going to do something
                I've never done before. (*Crosses to door* L.C.,
                locks it and takes key.)

MYRTLE   Mother, what did you mean just now when
                you said it wasn't Uncle Elwood's fault? If it's
                not his fault, whose fault is it?

VETA   Never you mind. I know whose fault it is.
                Now, lift up your head and smile and go
                back in as though nothing had happened.

MYRTLE   (*Crossing to doorway* D.R.) Oh, you're no match
                for Uncle Elwood!

VETA   You'll see.

                (*On her way out* MYRTLE *meets* ELWOOD *coming
                in.*)

MYRTLE   (*As they cross at door*) Mother's waiting for you.
                (*She exits* D.R.)

VETA   (*At* C.) Oh, Elwood!

ELWOOD   Yes, dear? Excuse me, Harvey.

VETA   Elwood, would you mind sitting down in here
                and waiting for me until the party is over.
                I've something to say to you – it's very
                important.

ELWOOD   (*Crossing to fireplace*) Of course. I've got some
                spare time and you're welcome to all of it.
                Oh, by the way – do you want Harvey to
                wait?

VETA   (*Very seriously, from doorway* D.R.) Yes, Elwood,
                I certainly do!

                (VETA *exits* D.R., *shutting the doors after her, and
                we hear them locked.*)

ELWOOD   (*To* HARVEY, *indicating chair* R.C.) Well, stick
around, old thing. (*He turns back to bookcase,*
L., *and as he does his eye lights on the whisky
decanter.*) Oh – h'm – yes . . . (*He picks up the
decanter and turns with it towards the chair.*)
Harvey, would you care for a snifter? No?
Oh! Oh, very well. (*He turns back to replace the
decanter, then turns again to chair, as though
someone had addressed him.*) What? Eh? (*He
looks around searching for something, then catches
sight of a mass of green leaves in the fireplace.*)
Oh! No – no – that isn't lettuce! (*He selects a
book from the bookcase, then goes* U.S. *and fetches
chair from beside door* L.C. *He brings the chair*
D.S. *and places it beside the armchair* R.C. *in
which* HARVEY *appears to be seated.*) Now,
Harvey, Veta wants to talk to us. She says it's
important. I expect she wants to congratulate
us on the impression we made at the party.
Oh, but we did! Yes, a great impression.
(*Sits.*) Now, would you like me to read you a
little of this? This? "Pride and Prejudice." But
you liked "Sense and Sensibility" – same
author. Or authoress. (*He crosses his left leg
over his right, knocking* HARVEY.) Oh, sorry, old
fellow! I didn't mean to kick you. Now then.
(*He reads from the book, and as he reads the
lighting fades until the stage is in darkness.*)
"Chapter one. It is a truth universally
acknowledged, that a single man in
possession of a good fortune should be in
want of a wife. . . ."

(*The stage is now in darkness* AND THE CURTAIN
FALLS)

END OF SCENE 1

SCENE 2

TIME: *An hour after the curtain of Scene 1.*

SET: *It is the office in the main building of Chumley's Rest – a sanatorium for mental patients. The wall at the back is half plaster with a large window. There is a door U.C. Through the door we can see the corridor of the sanatorium itself and the beginning of a staircase leading up to the wards. In the wall on stage R. is a door lettered "DR CHUMLEY." In the wall on stage L. are two doors, the U.S. door lettered "DR SANDERSON." The D.S. door leads to the outside of the sanatorium. There is a large desk L., with chairs L. and R. of it, and a small table R. with chairs L. and R. of it. There is a combined bookcase and filing cabinet U.S.R., and a single chair U.S.C. There is a pedestal ashtray between the doors, L.*

AT RISE: MISS RUTH KELLY, *head nurse at Chumley's Rest, is seated L. of desk, and* VETA R. *of desk.* KELLY *is a very pretty young woman of about twenty-four years. She is wearing a starched white uniform and cap. She is taking notes as she talks to* VETA. *The double doors, U.C., are open, the others shut.*

KELLY   (*Writing*) Mrs O. R. Simmons, 343, Temple Drive. Is that right?

VETA   We were born and raised there. It's old, but we love it. It's our home.

KELLY   And you wish to enter your brother here at the sanatorium for treatment. Your brother's name?

VETA   It's...Oh dear...(*She rises and crosses to table R. Her bag is on the table. Takes handkerchief from bag and dabs her eyes with it.*)

KELLY   Mrs Simmons, what is your bother's name?

VETA   I'm sorry. Life is not easy for any of us. I'll have to hold up my head and keep on just the same. That's what I keep telling Myrtle Mae, and that's what Myrtle Mae keeps on telling me. She's heartbroken about her Uncle Elwood. ... Oh. ... (*Crosses towards* KELLY) Elwood ... Elwood P. Dowd. (*Sits* R. *of desk.*)

KELLY   (*Writing*) Elwood P. Dowd. And his age?

VETA   Forty-seven the twenty-fourth of last April.

KELLY   Forty-seven; and is he married?

VETA   No, Elwood never married. He stayed with Mother. He was a great home boy. (*Sobbing.*) He loved his home.

KELLY   You have him with you now?

VETA   He's in a taxicab down in the driveway.

             (KELLY *rings the buzzer on* U.S. *end of desk.*)

             I gave the driver a dollar to watch him.

             (KELLY *crosses towards the filing cabinet.*)

             I didn't tell the man why – you can't tell these things to perfect strangers.

             (*Enter* WILSON, U.C. *He is a big, burly attendant about twenty-eight years old.* KELLY *turns and addresses him.*)

KELLY   Oh, Wilson, would you step down to a taxi in the driveway and ask a Mr Dowd if he would be good enough to step up to room No. 24, South Wing G?

WILSON   Ask him?

KELLY   (*Indicating* MRS SIMMONS *warningly*) This is his sister, Mrs Simmons.

WILSON   How do? Why certainly – (*Coming* D.S. *and below desk.*) I – um...I'd be glad to escort him.

             (*He gives* VETA *a suspicious look and exits* D.L. KELLY *has taken a printed card from the filing cabinet and crosses to* VETA *with it.*)

KELLY	The rates here, Mrs Simmons, you'll find printed on this card.
VETA	(*Waving it away*) That will all be taken care of by my mother's estate. Judge Gaffney is our attorney.
KELLY	(*Straightening her hair and dress*) Now I'll just see if Dr Sanderson can see you. (*Starts* U.L.)
VETA	What Dr Sanderson? I want to see Dr Chumley himself.
KELLY	Oh, Mrs Simmons, Dr Sanderson is the one who sees everybody. Dr Chumley sees no one.
VETA	He's still head of this institution, isn't he? He's still a psychiatrist, isn't he?
KELLY	Still a psychiatrist! Dr Chumley is more than that. He's a psychiatrist with a national reputation. Whenever people have mental breakdowns they start thinking of Dr Chumley.
VETA	(*Pointing* D.R.) That's his office, isn't it?
KELLY	Yes.
VETA	Well, you march straight in there and tell him I want to see him. When he knows who's here he'll come out here.
KELLY	But I wouldn't dare disturb him, Mrs Simmons. I'd be discharged if I did.
VETA	Well, I don't want to be pushed off on to any second fiddle.
KELLY	(*Warmly*) Dr Sanderson is nobody's second fiddle. He's very young, of course, and he hasn't been out of medical school very long, but Dr Chumley considers him the very best he's ever had out here. Dr Chumley tried out twelve and kept Dr Sanderson. He's really wonderful…(*Catches herself.*) Er – to the patients.

VETA	Very well, tell him I'm here.
KELLY	Right away. (*She picks up from the desk the form on which she has taken down the particulars and exits* U.L.)
	(VETA *crosses to table* R. *for compact and is powdering her nose as* WILSON *and* ELWOOD *enter* C.)
ELWOOD	Oh, Veta, isn't this a wonderful place?
	(WILSON *jerks him back and takes him off* C. *upstairs.* VETA *is still jumpy and nervous from the surprise, and her back is to the door* U.L. *as* DR SANDERSON *enters from it.* LYMAN SANDERSON *is a good-looking young man of about twenty-seven. He is wearing a starched white coat over dark trousers. He is holding the form which* KELLY *took off, and glances at it as he enters. He crosses to* VETA, *who is unaware of his entrance. She is still busy with the compact.* KELLY *enters behind* SANDERSON, *goes straight to doors* C. *and exits, closing doors behind her.*)
SANDERSON	(*Loudly*) Mrs Simmons?
VETA	(*Startled, she jumps*) Oh – dear – I didn't hear you come in. You startled me. You're – Dr Sanderson?
SANDERSON	That's right. Won't you be seated, please?
VETA	(*Sits chair* L. *of table* R.) Thank you. I hope you don't think I'm jumpy like that all the time, doctor.
SANDERSON	(*Crossing behind table of chair* R.) Of course not. Miss Kelly tells me you're concerned about your brother. Dowd, is it? Elwood P Dowd?
VETA	Yes doctor. He... This isn't easy for me, doctor.
SANDERSON	Naturally. These things aren't easy for the families of patients. I understand.

VETA · It's what Elwood's doing to himself, doctor, that's the trouble. Myrtle Mae has the right to nice friends. She's young and her whole life is before her. That's my daughter.

SANDERSON · Ah, your daughter. Mrs Simmons, when did you first begin to notice any peculiarity in you brother's actions?

VETA · I noticed it right away when Mother died and Myrtle and I came back home to live with Elwood. I could see then that he...that he...(*Twists handkerchief, looking pleadingly at doctor.*)

SANDERSON · That he – what? Take your time. Don't strain. Let it come. I'll wait for it.

VETA · Doctor – everything I say to you is confidential?

SANDERSON · Of course – that's understood.

VETA · Because it's a slap in the face of everything we've stood for in this community, the way Elwood is acting now.

SANDERSON · I'm not a gossip, Mrs Simmons – I'm a psychiatrist.

VETA · Oh, are you? Oh, yes, of course you are. Well – for one thing – he drinks.

SANDERSON · To excess?

VETA · To excess? (*Rises and walks to and fro.*) Don't you call it excess when a man never lets a day go by without stepping into one of those cheap taverns, sitting around with riffraff and people you've never heard of? Inviting them to the house, playing cards with them and giving them food and money? And here am I trying to get Myrtle Mae started with a nice group of young people. Well, if that's not excess, I'm sure I don't know what excess is!

SANDERSON   I didn't doubt your statement, Mrs Simmons.
             I merely asked if your brother drinks.

VETA   Well, then, I say definitely Elwood drinks.
             And I want him taken in here permanently,
             because I can not stand another day of that
             Harvey. (*Sits.*) Myrtle and I have to lay a
             place at the table for Harvey. We have to
             move over on the sofa and make room for
             Harvey. We have to answer the telephone
             when Elwood rings up and asks to speak to
             Harvey. Then at the party this afternoon,
             with Mrs. Chauvenet there...Why, we didn't
             even know anything about Harvey till we
             came back here. Don't you think, doctor, it
             would have been a little kinder of Mother to
             have written me about Harvey? Be honest
             now, don't you?

SANDERSON   Well, I really couldn't answer that question,
             Mrs Simmons.

VETA   Well, I can. Yes – it certainly would have!

SANDERSON   This person you call Harvey – who is he?

VETA   He's a rabbit!

SANDERSON   (*Patiently*) Perhaps – but just who is he? Some
             companion? – someone your brother picked
             up in one of those bars – of whom you
             disapprove?

VETA   Doctor – I've been telling you. Harvey is a
             rabbit. A big white rabbit. Six feet high...or
             is it six feet one and a half? Heaven knows, I
             ought to know – he's been around the house
             long enough.

             (SANDERSON *rises, perplexed.*)

SANDERSON   (*From* U.S. *of table*) Now, Mrs Simmons, let me
             just get this quite clear....

VETA   (*Impatiently*) Doctor, do I have to keep
            repeating myself? My brother insists that his
            closest friend is this big white rabbit. This
            rabbit is named Harvey. Don't you
            understand? Harvey lives at our house. He
            and Elwood go everywhere together. Elwood
            buys railway tickets and theatre tickets for
            Harvey. As I told Myrtle Mae, "If your uncle
            was so lonesome he had to bring something
            home, why couldn't he bring something
            human?" He's got me hasn't he? He's got
            Myrtle Mae, hasn't he? Doctor. (*She indicates
            the chair opposite and* SANDERSON *sits down
            again.* VETA *looks cautiously round the room.*)
            Doctor – I'm going to tell you something I've
            never told anybody in this world before.
            Every once in a while I see that big white
            rabbit myself! Now isn't that terrible? I've
            never even told that to Myrtle Mae.

SANDERSON   (*Rising*) Mrs Simmons ...

VETA   (*Rising*) And what's more he's every bit as big
            as Elwood says he is. Now don't tell that to a
            soul, doctor – I'm ashamed of it.

SANDERSON   Mrs Simmons, I can see that you have been
            suffering under a great strain recently.

VETA   Yes, I certainly have.

            (SANDERSON *crosses to* U.S *of desk.*)

SANDERSON   (*As he moves*) Grief over your mother's death
            has depressed you considerably?

VETA   Nobody knows how much. (*She moves to chair
            R. of desk and stands by it.*)

SANDERSON   Been losing sleep?

VETA   How could anybody sleep with all that going
            on? (*Sits.*)

SANDERSON   Short-tempered over trifles?

VETA   You just try living with those two and see
                 how your temper holds out.

SANDERSON   (*Presses buzzer*) Loss of appetite?

VETA   No one could eat at a table with my brother
                 and a big white rabbit.

                 (SANDERSON *presses buzzer again.*)

                 Well, I'm finished with it.

                 (SANDERSON *is repeatedly pressing buzzer. No one
                 comes. He looks out with annoyance into the hall
                 through doors* U.C. *he presses the buzzer again,
                 then back to the doors.*)

                 I'll sell the house and be appointed trustee of
                 Elwood's estate, and Myrtle Mae and I will be
                 able to entertain our friends in peace. (*She
                 breaks down.*) It's too much, doctor, I just can't
                 stand it.

SANDERSON   (*From* U.S. *of* VETA'S *chair, soothingly*) Yes, of
                 course Mrs Simmons, of course it is. (*She
                 nods.*) And now I'm going to help you. (*He
                 backs to the doorway* U.C., *watching her
                 cautiously.*) You just sit there quietly, Mrs
                 Simmons, and I'll be right back.

                 (*He exits* U.C., *closing the doors,* VETA *sits for a
                 few moments, sobbing and mumbling to herself.*)

VETA   Oh, doctor, I'll just go down to the cab and
                 get Elwood's things.

                 (*There is no reply. She looks round and realises she
                 is alone. She crosses to table* R. *picks up her bag,
                 then crosses towards door,* D.L.)

                 Now, which door did I come in at? (*She
                 wavers, then makes for door* D.L. *and exits.*)

SANDERSON   (*Off* C.) Now, why didn't someone answer the
                 buzzer? I rang and rang.

	(SANDERSON *enters* C., *followed by* KELLY *and* WILSON. *They stop when they see there is no one there.* SANDERSON *goes to door* U.L. *and looks into his office,* KELLY *looks off through door* D.L., *leaving it open.*)
SANDERSON	Mrs Simmons!
KELLY	(*At door* D.L.) Mrs Simmons!
SANDERSON	Sound the gong, Wilson. That poor woman must not leave the grounds.
	(WILSON *runs to panel set in bookcase and starts the alarm bell.*)
WILSON	She made a getaway, eh, Doc.?
SANDERSON	(L. *of desk*) Her condition is serious. Go after her.
	(*Exit* WILSON U.C. KELLY *crosses to bookcase, switches off alarm and closes panel.*)
	(*Speaking into dictaphone on desk.*) Henry!
MALE VOICE	(*Through dictaphone speaker, from microphone, off*) Main gate.
SANDERSON	Henry, allow no one out of the main gates, we're looking for a patient.
MALE VOICE	All right, doctor, I'll lock them.
SANDERSON	(*To* KELLY) I ought never to have left her alone, but no one answered the buzzer.
KELLY	(*Crossing towards desk*) Wilson was in South, doctor.
SANDERSON	Now what have we available, Miss Kelly?
KELLY	Number 13, Upper West R, is ready, doctor.
SANDERSON	Then have her taken there immediately, and I'll prescribe preliminary treatment. Now I must contact her brother. (*Picks up telephone directory.*) Dowd's the name. Elwood P Dowd. (*He starts looking through the directory, then gives it up and pushes the directory over to* KELLY.) Get him on the telephone, will you, Kelly?

KELLY   (*Moving up to* R. *of desk*) But, doctor, I didn't
             know it was the woman who needed the
             treatment. She said it was for her brother.

SANDERSON   Of course she did. It's the oldest dodge in the
             world – always used by a cunning type of
             psychopath. She apparently knew her brother
             was going to commit her, so she came out
             first to discredit him. Now, get him on the
             telephone, Kelly.

KELLY   But, doctor, I thought the woman was all
             right – so I had Wilson take the brother up
             to No. 24, South Wing G. He's there now.

SANDERSON   (*Horrified*) You had Wilson take the brother.
             Now, no jokes, please, Miss Kelly. (*He bends
             over the form on the desk then looks up again.*)
             You're not serious?

KELLY   Oh, I did, doctor, I did! Oh, doctor, I'm
             terribly sorry.

SANDERSON   Oh, well, if you're sorry, that fixes
             everything. Now really, Miss Kelly ... (*He
             starts for dictaphone.*)

KELLY   Oh, I'll do it, doctor.

             (KELLY *goes to dictaphone, and* SANDERSON
             crosses to window and looks out.)

KELLY   (*Into dictaphone*) Dunphy!

FEMALE
VOICE   Yes, Miss Kelly?

KELLY   Will you please unlock the door to Number
             24 and give Mr Dowd his clothes.... (*She
             looks up at* SANDERSON.)

SANDERSON   Ask him to step down to the office right
             away.

KELLY   (*Into dictaphone*) And ask him to step down to
             the office right away. There's been a terrible
             mistake and Dr Sanderson wants to
             explain...

FEMALE VOICE	O.K., Miss Kelly.
SANDERSON	Explain? Apologise! (*He comes down* R. *of table, then crosses towards* C.)
KELLY	(*From desk*) Thank heavens they hadn't put him in a hydro-tub yet. She'll let him out.
SANDERSON	(*Staring at her*) Beautiful and dumb too. It's almost too good to be true.
KELLY	(*Crossing to* C.) Doctor, I feel terrible.

(SANDERSON *moves towards her, then turns away and goes back to window, looking out.*)

I didn't know. Judge Gaffney called and said Mrs Simmons and her brother would be coming out here. She seemed quite normal, and ... (*She breaks off.*) Well, you don't have to be rude!

SANDERSON	Oh, don't I? Now, stop worrying. We'll squirm out of it some way – I hope! (*Thinking, he starts toward* R.)
KELLY	Where are you going?
SANDERSON	I've got to tell the chief about it, Kelly. He may want to handle this himself.
KELLY	(*Following* SANDERSON *and stopping* R.C.) He'll be furious. I know he will. He'll die! And then he'll terminate me.
SANDERSON	The responsibility is all mine, Miss Kelly. (*Going to door* R.)
KELLY	Oh no, doctor, tell him it was all my fault.
SANDERSON	(*At door*) I never mention your name – except in my sleep.
KELLY	But this man Dowd?
SANDERSON	Don't let him get away – I'll be right back. (*Turns to open door.*)

KELLY But what shall I say to him? What shall I do? He'll be furious.

SANDERSON (*Turning two steps back into room*) Look, Kelly, he'll probably be fit to burst – but he's a man, isn't he?

KELLY I guess so – his name's mister.

SANDERSON And you're a woman. Well – use your wits – use your eyes – use your...use your influence. But keep him here.

(*Exits* D.R.)

KELLY (*Very angry, speaking to closed door*) Well, of all the ... Oh you're wonderful, Dr Sanderson! You're just about the most wonderful person I ever met in my life. (*Folds arms.*)

(WILSON *enters* C. *just in time to hear the last sentence.*)

WILSON Sure! But how about giving me a lift here just the same?

KELLY (*Turning*) What?

WILSON That Simmons dame.

KELLY (*Crosses to* WILSON) Did you catch her?

WILSON Slick as a whistle! She was comin' along the path hummin' a little tune. I jumps out at her from behind a tree. I say "Sister, there's a man want to see you." Shoulda heard her yell – she's crazy all right!

KELLY Well, take her to Number 13, Upper West R.

WILSON She's there now. I brought her in through the diet kitchen. She's screamin' and kickin' like hell. I'll hold her if you'll come and undress her.

KELLY (*Crossing* WILSON *to* L. *of desk*) Just a minute, Wilson. Dr Sanderson told me to stay till her brother comes down.

WILSON	Well make it snappy, will you? (*Exit* U.C.)
KELLY	(*Switches on dictaphone*) Dunphy, where is Mr Dowd?
	(ELWOOD *enters* U.C. *from staircase. He is wearing his own hat and carrying* HARVEY's *hat and coat.*)
KELLY	Oh, it's all right, Dunphy.
	(KELLY *switches off and moves toward* ELWOOD.)
	You're Mr Dowd?
ELWOOD	(*Seeing her, he bows*) Elwood P. Let me give you one of my cards. (*Produces pile of cards from pocket.*) If you should want me, call at that number.
KELLY	(*Looking at card*) Charlie's place?
ELWOOD	It's a bar – but they'll call me. And don't worry should you lose it – I have plenty more.
KELLY	I'm Miss Kelly. Won't you have a chair please, Mr Dowd? (*Indicating chair* L. *of table* R.)
	(KELLY *goes to doors* U.C. *and closes them.* ELWOOD "*sees*" HARVEY *enter* D.L.)
ELWOOD	Oh, there you are. (*To* KELLY.) Thank you – I'll have two.
	(ELWOOD *brings another chair from* U.C. *and places it next to chair* L. *of table* R. *He places* HARVEY's *hat and coat on table, then turns to* KELLY.)
KELLY	(*Coming down from doors*) Dr Sanderson is very anxious to talk to you, Mr Dowd. He'll be here in a minute. Won't you sit down?
ELWOOD	(*Bowing*) After you, Miss Kelly.

KELLY	Oh, really, I can't, thank you. I'm in and out all the time. but you mustn't mind me. Please sit down.
ELWOOD	(*Bowing*) After you.

(KELLY *sits chair* R. *of desk.* ELWOOD *sits on the chair* C. *that he has placed in position. They look at one another in embarrassed silence for a few moments.*)

KELLY	Could I get you a magazine to look at?
ELWOOD	I would rather look at you, if you don't mind, Miss Kelly. You are very lovely.
KELLY	Oh – er – thank you. Some people don't seem to think so.

(*Enter* SANDERSON *from* D.R. *just in time to hear the last remark.*)

ELWOOD	(*He does see* SANDERSON) Some people are blind. That's often brought to my attention. And now I must introduce you to ...
SANDERSON	(*Going to him and extending hand*) Mr Dowd?
ELWOOD	Ah! Elwood P. Let me give you one of my cards. (*Handing card.*) If you should want ...
SANDERSON	(*Crossing* ELWOOD *to* C.) Mr Dowd, I am Dr Lyman Sanderson, Dr Chumley's assistant out here.
ELWOOD	Ah, good for you! I'm happy to know you. And how are you, doctor?
SANDERSON	I'm very well, thank you, Mr Dowd.
ELWOOD	Really! Must be something you ate!

SANDERSON   Won't you sit down? You've met Miss Kelly here?

ELWOOD   I've had that great pleasure. And now I want you both to meet a very dear friend of mine. . . .

SANDERSON   (*Interrupting him*) Later on – be glad to. But, first of all, won't you sit down?

ELWOOD   After Miss Kelly.

SANDERSON   (*Waving to* KELLY *to sit*) Oh, sit down, Kelly.

(KELLY *sits chair* L. *of desk,* ELWOOD *sits* C., *placing his hat beneath chair. As he sits,* ELWOOD *motions to* HARVEY *to sit in the chair beside him.*)

Is that chair quite comfortable, Mr Dowd?

ELWOOD   Yes, thank you, doctor. (*Half rising.*) Would you care to try it?

SANDERSON   (*Motions him to sit*) No thank you, Mr Dowd.

ELWOOD   Oh . . . very well. (*Sits and produces cigarette case.*) Do you mind if I smoke?

SANDERSON   Of course not, Mr Dowd. You'd like an ash-tray. Miss Kelly, could we get Mr Dowd an ash-tray?

(KELLY *fetches an ash-tray from* L. *of desk and takes it to* ELWOOD, *who places it between him and* HARVEY.)

SANDERSON   (*Crossing to window*) Is it too warm in here; shall I open a window?

(ELWOOD *does not hear* SANDERSON. *He is looking at* KELLY, *who has backed to* D.S. *of desk. here is silence for a moment.*)

Kelly   Mr Dowd – Dr Sanderson wants to know if he should open a window.

ELWOOD   Well, that's up to him, isn't it? I wouldn't presume to live his life for him.

(During the following dialogue ELWOOD *exchanges glances and laughs with* HARVEY *as appropriate. From time to time he nudges* HARVEY *and moves as though* HARVEY *had nudged him back. At these moments* SANDERSON *and* KELLY *are looking at each other, so that they do not see the by-play.* SANDERSON *comes to* C., *facing* ELWOOD. KELLY *sits chair* L. *of desk.)*

SANDERSON   Mr Dowd, I can see that you're not the type of person to be taken in by any high-flown phrases or beating about the bush.

ELWOOD   Is that so, doctor?

SANDERSON   You have us at a disadvantage here. You know it, and we know it. Let's lay our cards on the table.

Elwood   *(Rises and moves toward desk, producing pack of cards from pocket)* Well, that certainly appeals to me!

SANDERSON   I was only speaking figuratively, Mr Dowd.

ELWOOD   *(Putting cards away)* Oh, figuratively? I see. *(Sits.)* A pity.

SANDERSON   It pays to be frank in the long run. After all, people are people no matter where you go.

ELWOOD   That is very often the case.

SANDERSON   And, being human, they are therefore liable to mistakes. Miss Kelly and I have made a mistake out here this afternoon, Mr Dowd, and we'd like to explain it to you.

KELLY	It wasn't Dr Sanderson's fault, Mr Dowd; it was mine.
SANDERSON	A human failing – as I said.
ELWOOD	Nevertheless I find it very interesting. I mean . . . you and Miss Kelly . . . here . . . this afternoon . . .
KELLY	We do hope you'll understand, Mr Dowd.
ELWOOD	Of course. These things are often the basis of a long and warm friendship.
SANDERSON	And the responsibility is, of course . . . not hers, but mine.
ELWOOD	Indeed? Your attitude may be old-fashioned, doctor, but I like it.
SANDERSON	Now, if I had seen your sister first, that would have been an entirely different matter.
	(ELWOOD and HARVEY *are overcome with amusement.*)
ELWOOD	You really do surprise me, doctor. I think the world of my sister – but I should have imagined that she had seen her day.
SANDERSON	You mustn't attach any blame on her – she's a very sick woman. Came in here insisting you were in need of treatment. Well, of course, that's perfectly ridiculous.
ELWOOD	Oh, Veta shouldn't be upset about me. I get along fine.
SANDERSON	Exactly – but your sister has already talked to Miss Kelly here, and there had been a call from your family solicitor, Judge Gaffney . . .

ELWOOD   Oh yes, I know the judge. Know his wife too.
            Beautiful woman. He's a very good judge.
            (*He fumbles in his pockets.*)

SANDERSON   Is there something I can get for you, Mr
            Dowd?

ELWOOD   What did you have in mind?

SANDERSON   Well – how about a light for your cigarette?

ELWOOD   Well – that's one idea.

            (SANDERSON *produces lighter, crosses to* ELWOOD
            and lights cigarette for him. ELWOOD *takes a deep
            puff at the cigarette and blows a great cloud of
            smoke in front of the empty chair beside him.*
            SANDERSON *has turned back to the desk.*)

            Oh, sorry, old fellow! Thoughtless of me.

SANDERSON   (*Sitting chair* R. *of desk*) Your sister was
            extremely nervous and began a heated tirade
            on your drinking.

ELWOOD   That was Veta.

SANDERSON   She became hysterical.

ELWOOD   Oh, Veta shouldn't worry about my drinking.
            I take care of that.

SANDERSON   Exactly. I suppose you take a drink now and
            then, Mr Dowd – like the rest of us?

ELWOOD   As a matter of fact, I do. As a matter of fact
            (*emphatically*) I could do with one right now.

SANDERSON   As a matter of fact – so could I!

ELWOOD   Well – we're all getting very matter of fact,
            aren't we?

SANDERSON   Your sister's reaction to the whole matter of
            drinking was entirely too intense. Does your
            sister drink, Mr Dowd?

ELWOOD   Oh no. I don't think I've ever known Veta
              take a drink.

SANDERSON   Well, I'm going to surprise you; because I
              think she has and does – constantly.

ELWOOD   You certainly do surprise me, doctor. . . .

SANDERSON   But it's not her alcoholism that's going to
              form the basis for my diagnosis. It's more
              serious than that. It was when she began
              talking so emotionally about this big white
              rabbit – Harvey – yes (*turning to* KELLY), I
              believe she called him Harvey?

ELWOOD   Harvey is his name.

              (SANDERSON *and* KELLY *look at him, a little
              puzzled.*)

SANDERSON   She claimed you were persecuting her with
              this Harvey.

ELWOOD   I wouldn't persecute Veta with Harvey – she
              shouldn't look at it like that. And now, before
              we go any further, I must introduce you . . .
              (*Rises.*)

SANDERSON   (*Rising and motioning to* ELWOOD *to sit down
              again*) Let me make my point first, Mr Dowd.

ELWOOD   . . . Make your point first. (*Sits.*)

SANDERSON   This trouble of your sister's didn't spring up
              overnight. Her condition stems from trauma.

ELWOOD   From what?

SANDERSON   Trauma. It's spelt t-r-a-u-m-a. It means
              shock. There's nothing unusual about it.
              There's – there's the birth trauma; that's the
              shock of the act of being born.

ELWOOD   That's the one we never get over!

              (*They all laugh.*)

SANDERSON   You have a unique sense of humour, Mr
              Dowd – hasn't he, Miss Kelly?

KELLY   Oh yes, doctor.

ELWOOD   Thank you, my dear; may I say the same for
              both of you?

SANDERSON   To sum it all up, Mr Dowd, your sister's
              condition is serious – but I can help her. She
              must, however, remain out here –
              temporarily of course.

ELWOOD   Oh, wait. I've always wanted Veta to have
              everything she needs. But I wouldn't want
              her to stay out here unless she liked it out
              here and wanted to stay here.

SANDERSON   Of course. (*Turns to* KELLY.) Did Wilson get
              what he went after?

KELLY   Yes, doctor. (*She rises.*)

SANDERSON   What was Mrs Simmons' attitude, Kelly?

KELLY   Not unusual, doctor. (*She crosses to filing
              cabinet* R.)

SANDERSON   (*Turning back to* ELWOOD) Mr Dowd, if this
              were some ordinary delusion – something
              reflected on the memory picture – in other
              words, if this were something she had seen
              once before – that would be one thing. But
              this is more serious. It stands to reason
              nobody has ever seen a white rabbit six feet
              high.

ELWOOD   Not very often!

(ELWOOD *and* SANDERSON *both laugh heartily.*
SANDERSON *turns back to desk and fiddles with the*
papers on it. KELLY *is busy at the filing cabinet.*
ELWOOD *nudges* HARVEY *vigorously, and*
apparently HARVEY *nudges him still more*
vigorously, for ELWOOD *is knocked out of his chair*
on to the floor. He gets up and sits down again.
SANDERSON *turns to him.*)

SANDERSON   I like you, Dowd!

ELWOOD   And I like you too, doctor; and Miss Kelly
              here – (*Turning towards her.*) I like her too.

              (KELLY *turns towards him.*)

SANDERSON   Not often is right! So, you see, she must
              remain out here temporarily. Under these
              circumstances I would commit my own
              grandmother.

ELWOOD   Why – does your grandmother drink?

SANDERSON   That's just another figure of speech, Mr
              Dowd. (*Sits* L. *of desk.*) Now, will you sign
              these papers as next of kin? It's just a
              formality.

ELWOOD   (*Rises and crosses to desk*) Oh, wait. I think we'd
              better have Veta do that. She does all the
              signing for the family. She's good at it.

SANDERSON   We can't disturb her now.

ELWOOD   Well, I'd better talk it over with Judge
              Gaffney.

SANDERSON   You can explain it all to him later. Say I
              advised it. It isn't as though you couldn't look
              in here any time and make inquiries. I'll
              make out a full visitor's pass for you. (*Writes*
              on card.)

ELWOOD   Will you do that, doctor? (*Sits* R. *of desk.*)

SANDERSON   Glad to have you. When would you like to
                 come back? Wednesday, say – or Friday?

ELWOOD   Well, as you and Miss Kelly have both been
                 so pleasant, I could come back right after
                 dinner.

SANDERSON   Well, we're pretty busy round here – but I
                 expect that'll be all right.

ELWOOD   Well, I needn't go now. I'm not very hungry.

SANDERSON   Delighted to have you stay. But Miss Kelly
                 and I have to get on upstairs now – we've got
                 lots of work to do. But I'll tell you what you
                 might like to do, sir.

ELWOOD   What might I like to do, sir?

SANDERSON   Well, we don't usually do this – but just to
                 make sure in your own mind that your sister
                 is in good hands – why don't you have a look
                 around? If you go through this door (*rises
                 and opens doors* C.) and turn right, you'll find
                 the occupational therapy room, and beyond
                 that the library and the diet kitchen. (*He is
                 holding the visitor's pass.*)

ELWOOD   (*Rising*) Well, perhaps for Veta's sake I'd
                 better do that.

SANDERSON   (*Facing* ELWOOD U.S.C.) And I must say I've
                 enjoyed having this little talk with you, Mr
                 Dowd.

ELWOOD   And I've enjoyed it too, doctor, meeting you
                 and Miss Kelly here.

                 (KELLY *stands just below and to* R. *of table,
                 holding some documents she has taken from the
                 filing cabinet.*)

SANDERSON   And I will say that for a layman you show an
             unusually acute perception into psychiatric
             problems.

ELWOOD   Is that so, doctor? I didn't think I knew
             anything about it. I mean, nobody does, do
             you think?

SANDERSON   Well – the good psychiatrist is not found
             under every bush.

ELWOOD   Oh no – you have to pick the right bush!
             Now – since we all seem to be enjoying
             ourselves so much – let's keep right on with
             it. I'd like to invite you both down to
             Charlie's place to have a drink. When I enjoy
             people I like to stay right with them.

SANDERSON   I'm afraid we're on duty now, Mr Dowd; but
             some other time – be glad to.

ELWOOD   When – would you be glad to?

SANDERSON   Well, I couldn't say right now. You see, Miss
             Kelly and I don't go off duty till ten o'clock
             tonight.

ELWOOD   Then we'll all go down to Charlie's place at
             ten o'clock tonight!

SANDERSON   I'm afraid that's not possible, Mr Dowd.

ELWOOD   Oh – why not?

SANDERSON   Doctor Chumley doesn't approve of members
             of the staff fraternising.

ELWOOD   Oh ... miserable old so-and-so! ...

SANDERSON   But – since you've been so understanding –
             perhaps we could manage it. (*Hands "visitor's
             pass" card to* ELWOOD.)

ELWOOD   That's settled, then – I'll pick you up here in
             a cab at ten o'clock tonight, and the four of
             us will have a happy evening. I want you
             both to become friends with a very dear
             friend of mine. "Later on," you said – later

on it shall be. Miss Kelly, your servant. Dr
Sanderson, your friend. (*He bows to* KELLY,
shakes hand with SANDERSON, *and moves up to
door* C., *inserting "visitor's pass" in the band of
his hat as he goes. He turns in the doorway and
waves again.*) A toute á l'heure! (*Then, leaning
confidentially towards* SANDERSON, *who followed
him to the door.*) I say, doc., that was a good
one about the bush!

(*Laughing, he puts on his hat, showing the card
pushed into the band, and exits.*)

KELLY   (*She drops the documents she had been holding on
to the table and replaces the chair which* ELWOOD
had brought forward) Whew – now I can
breath again!

SANDERSON   (*Shuts doors and move to* L. *of desk*) That was a
close shave all right, but he seemed to be a
pretty reasonable sort of fellow. You know,
Kelly, that man is proud. What he had to be
proud of I don't know – but I played up to
that pride. You can get to almost anybody if
you want to. And now I'd better look in on
that Simmons woman. (*Starts to cross* U.C.
KELLY *comes towards him.*)

KELLY   Dr Sanderson!

(*He stops. They are facing each other in front of
the doors* U.C.)

KELLY   You say you can get to anybody if you want
to. How can you do that?

SANDERSON   Oh, takes study, Kelly. Years and years of
specialised training. you know – there's only
one thing I don't like about this Dowd
business.

KELLY   What's that?

SANDERSON   Having to make that date with him. Of
             course, that man has left here as a good
             friend and booster of this sanatorium, so I
             suppose there's no harm in it – but you don't
             have to go.

KELLY   Oh?

SANDERSON   There's no point in it. I'll have a drink with
             him, pat him on the back and then leave.
             (*Going to* L. *of desk.*) I've got a date tonight
             anyway – I think.

KELLY   Oh, by all means. (*Elaborately casual, she picks
             up the ash-tray and places it* U.S.C.) I didn't
             intend to go anyway. The idea bores me stiff.
             (*Getting worked up.*) I wouldn't go if I never
             went anywhere again! I wouldn't go – if my
             whole life depended on it!

             (*She folds her arms and crosses to window, her
             back to* SANDERSON.)

SANDERSON   Whatever is the matter with you, Miss Kelly?
             What are you getting so emotional about?

KELLY   (*Turning*) Well, he may be a peculiar man
             with funny clothes; but *he* knows how to
             behave. *His* manners were perfect.

SANDERSON   I saw you getting off with him. I didn't miss
             all that.

KELLY   (*Coming to* C.) He wouldn't sit down till I sat
             down. He told me I was lovely, and he called
             me dear. I'd go and have a drink with him if
             you weren't going.

SANDERSON   (*Going to her*) Of course you would. And look
             at him – all he does is hang around bars! But
             you'd sit with and let him flatter you. You
             know, you're a lovely girl, Miss Kelly, but ...

KELLY   Now let me tell you ...

             (*This argument is interrupted by the entrance from
             D.R. of the great DR CHUMLEY. He is a large,
             handsome man of about fifty-seven. He has grey
             hair and is wearing glasses. He wears a starched
             white coat over dark trousers. His manner is
             confident, pompous and lordly. He is good and he
             knows it. He is carrying a book.*)

CHUMLEY   Dr Sanderson! Miss Kelly!

             (*They break apart and stand to attention.*)

KELLY and
SANDERSON   Yes, doctor!

CHUMLEY   (*Moving D.S. to front of table*) Tell the
             gardener to prune more carefully round
             those prize dahlias of mine – along the fence
             by the main road. They'll be ready for
             cutting (*he looks in book*) next week. (*He places
             book on top of bookcase.*) The difficulty of the
             woman who has the big white rabbit – has
             that all been smoothed over?

SANDERSON   Yes, doctor.

CHUMLEY   (*He produces handkerchief and begins polishing
             glasses*) While I have had many patients out
             here who saw animals, I have never before
             had a patient – with an animal – ha-ha! –
             that large.

SANDERSON   Yes, doctor – she called him "Harvey."

CHUMLEY   An unusual name for an animal of any kind. "Harvey" (*with the "H" of "Harvey" he breathes on his glasses, then resumes polishing*) is a man's name. I have known several men in my time named Harvey, but I have never heard of any type of animal whatsoever with that name.

SANDERSON   Yes, doctor. I mean no, doctor.

CHUMLEY   (*Going* U.S. *to* SANDERSON) I will go upstairs with you and look in on this woman. It may be that we can use my formula 977 on her. (*Putting his hand on* SANDERSON'S *shoulder.*) I'll give you my advice in prescribing treatment for her.

SANDERSON   Thank you, doctor.

CHUMLEY   (*Noticing the hat and coat placed on the table by* ELWOOD) And now may I ask – what is that hat and coat doing on this table? Whose is it?

SANDERSON   I don't know, sir. Do you know, Miss Kelly – was it Dowd's?

KELLY   (*Picking up hat and coat from table*) He had his hat on, doctor. Perhaps it belongs to the relative of one of the patients.

CHUMLEY   (*At* C.) Hand me that hat.

KELLY   (*Handing it*) Yes, doctor.

CHUMLEY   (*Looking inside*) No name inside. This type of hat has never appealed to me. I prefer a Homburg. (*Looks at it again.*) What's this? (*He pushes two fingers through holes cut in from of the crown of the hat.*) Two holes cut in the crown of this hat! See?

KELLY   That's strange!

CHUMLEY   Some new fad. Take them away – hang them
               up – get them out of here.

               (KELLY *takes them into room* U.L., SANDERSON
               crosses to desk, CHUMLEY *comes down to table and
               picks up the documents* KELLY *has left there. He is
               glancing at them when* WILSON *comes running on*
               C. WILSON *is very impressed with* DR CHUMLEY
               and very fond of him.)

WILSON   Hullo Dr Chumley! How's everything?

CHUMLEY   (*Dropping documents on table*) Fine, thank you,
               Wilson.

               (KELLY *re-enters* U.L.)

WILSON   Look – somebody's going to have to give me
               a hand with this Simmons dame – order a
               strait–jacket or something. She's terrible! (*To
               KELLY.*) Forgot me, didn't you? Well – I got
               her corset off all by myself!

CHUMLEY   We're going up to see this patient right now,
               Wilson.

WILSON   She's in the hydro-tub. My god – I left the
               water running on her!

               (*He runs off* U.C. *upstairs.*)

SANDERSON   You did what?

               (*Enter* BETTY CHUMLEY, *The doctor's wife. She is
               good-natured, fat and bustling, a grey-haired
               woman of about fifty-five.*)

BETTY   Good evening, Dr Sanderson!

SANDERSON   Good evening, Mrs Chumley!

	(SANDERSON *and* KELLY *run off after* WILSON U.C. *upstairs.*)

BETTY   (*Crossing to* C. *to* CHUMLEY) Willie, you haven't forgotton Dr McClure's cocktail party? We promised them faithfully.

CHUMLEY   That's right. I have to see a patient right now. Be down shortly. . . .

                 (*He exits* U.C. *upstairs.*)

BETTY   Oh, give a quick little diagnosis, Willie; we don't want to be late for the party. (*Turns and moves to window.*) I'm dying to see the inside of that house.

                 (*She looks out of the window as* ELWOOD *enters* U.C. *He does not see* BETTY; *he looks round the room.*)

ELWOOD   (*At* C., *looking* L.) 'Straordinary! (*He turns to* U.S. *and makes to exit again.*)

BETTY   Good evening!

ELWOOD   (*Removes hat and bows*) Oh – good evening!

BETTY   I'm Mrs Chumley – Dr Chumley's wife.

ELWOOD   I'm happy to know that. Dowd is my name, Elwood P. Dowd. Let me give you one of my cards. (*Gives her a card.*) If you should want me, call me at Charlie's place – I've been to Eddie's Bar.

BETTY   Thank you. (*She takes the card and sits rather nervously on chair* L. *of table.*) Is there something I can do for you?

ELWOOD   What did you have in mind?

BETTY   You – you seem to be looking for someone.

ELWOOD   I'm looking for Harvey. (*Crosses and looks of*
           D.L.) I went off without him. Silly of me.

BETTY   Harvey? Is he a patient here?

ELWOOD   (*Coming back to* C.) Oh no – nothing like that.

BETTY   Does he work here?

ELWOOD   No, Harvey doesn't work here. He's just my
           best friend. He's also a pooka. He came out
           with me and my sister Veta this afternoon.

BETTY   Where was he when you last saw him?

ELWOOD   (*Indicating chair on which she is sitting*) In that
           chair with his hat and coat on that table.

BETTY   Well, there doesn't seem to be any hat and
           coat around here now. Perhaps he's left.

ELWOOD   Apparently. (*Crossing and looking off* U.L.) I
           can't see him anywhere.

BETTY   What was that word you said just now –
           pooka?

ELWOOD   (*Crosses to* C.) Yes – that's it.

BETTY   Is that something new?

ELWOOD   Oh, no. As I understand it, it's something
           very old.

BETTY   Really? Well, I never happened to have
           heard it before.

ELWOOD   I'm not surprised at that. I hadn't run across
           it myself until I met him. I hope to have the
           pleasure of introducing you some time. I'm
           sure he would be quite taken with you.

BETTY   Oh, well – it's very nice of you to say so.

ELWOOD   Not at all. If Harvey takes a liking to people,
           he expresses himself quite definitely. But if
           he's not particularly interested, he'll sit – like
           an empty chair – or an empty space on the
           floor. Yes – Harvey takes his time making up
           his mind about people. Choosey, you might
           say.

BETTY   That's not such a bad way to be – in this day
           and age.

ELWOOD   Harvey is fond of my sister Veta. That's
           because he's fond of me – and my sister and
           I come from the same family. Now, you'd
           think that feeling would be mutual, wouldn't
           you? But Veta doesn't seem to care for
           Harvey. Don't you think that's rather too
           bad, Mrs Chumley?

BETTY   Oh, I don't know, Mr Dowd. I gave up a long
           time ago expecting my family to like my
           friends. It's useless.

ELWOOD   Well – we must keep on trying.

BETTY   There's no harm in trying.

ELWOOD   (*Crossing above table to* R. *of table*) Because if
           Harvey has said it to me once, he's said it to
           me a thousand times – "Mr Dowd, I would
           do anything for you." (*He imitates a rabbit with
           his mouth. Sitting on chair* R. *of table.*) Mrs
           Chumley –

BETTY   Yes –

ELWOOD	Did you know that Mrs MacElhinney's Aunt Rose is going to drop in on her unexpectedly tonight – from Cleveland?
BETTY	Why no – I didn't!
ELWOOD	Neither does she! – and that puts you both in the same boat, doesn't it?
BETTY	Well, I don't know anybody named Mrs. . . .
ELWOOD	Mrs MacElhinney? Lives next door to us. Wonderful woman. It was Harvey who told me about her Aunt Rose. Now that's an interesting little news item, isn't it, Mrs Chumley? – and as far as I know you are perfectly at liberty to pass it around.
BETTY	Well I . . .
ELWOOD	Mrs C – would you care to come downtown with me? I'd be so happy to buy you a drink.
BETTY	Well, thank you very much – but I'm waiting for Dr Chumley, and if he came down and found me gone, he'd be liable to raise h . . . He would be irritated.
ELWOOD	And we wouldn't want that, would we? Well – some other time perhaps. (*He rises and crosses to* C.)
BETTY	I'll tell you what I'll do, however.
ELWOOD	(*Turning*) What – will you do, however? I'm interested.
BETTY	If your friend comes in while I'm here, I'd be glad to give him a message for you.
ELWOOD	Would you be good enough to do that for me? Well, I certainly would appreciate that.
BETTY	No trouble at all. I'll write it down on the back of this card. (*Holds up card and takes pencil from purse.*) What would you like to tell him if he comes in while I'm still here?

ELWOOD   Just ask him to meet me downtown – if he
            has no other plans.

BETTY   (*Writing*) Meet Mr Dowd downtown. (*To*
            ELWOOD.) Any particular place downtown?

ELWOOD   He knows where. Harvey knows this town
            like a book.

BETTY   (*Writing*) Harvey – you know where. (*To*
            ELWOOD.) Harvey what?

ELWOOD   Oh – just Harvey.

BETTY   (*Rises and crosses to* L.C.) I'll tell you what!

ELWOOD   What?

BETTY   Doctor and I are going downtown – to
            Twelfth and Mount Drive. Dr McClure is
            having a cocktail party.

ELWOOD   (*Greatly interested, he writes on a scribbling-pad
            on the desk*) A cocktail party at Twelfth and
            Mount Drive. (*He tears the page off and folds it
            carefully.*) That's an interesting little news
            item, isn't it, Mrs Chumley? (*Puts note away in
            pocket.*)

BETTY   We're driving there in a few minutes. We
            could give your friend a lift.

ELWOOD   Well, I hate to impose on you, but I certainly
            would appreciate that.

BETTY   Oh, it's no trouble. Dr McClure is having this
            party for his sister – from Wichita.

ELWOOD   Oh! I didn't know Dr McClure had a sister in
            Wichita.

BETTY	Oh – then you know Dr McClure?
ELWOOD	No! Never heard of him!

(BETTY *looks startled.* ELWOOD *picks up his hat from the desk.*)

ELWOOD	Now, are you quite sure you haven't time to come and have a little drink?
BETTY	Oh, I really couldn't – but thank you all the same.
ELWOOD	Well – some other time perhaps. It's been a great pleasure to meet you, dear lady, and I hope we shall meet again quite soon. (*He raises her hand to kiss it, then catches sight of her wrist-watch.*) Twenty past five! Good night, my dear. (*He puts on his hat and make for door* D.L. *he stops, struck by a sudden thought, then returns to* BETTY.) Oh – silly of me. I forgot. You can't miss Harvey – he's tall, very tall. (*Raises his hands above his head, standing on tiptoe.*) Like that! (*Raises hat.*) Good night my dear. (*Replaces hat and exits* D.L.)

(BETTY *sits chair* R. *of desk, looking after* ELWOOD. *From* U.C. *down the stairs comes* CHUMLEY, *followed by* SANDERSON *and* KELLY. CHUMLEY *goes towards chair* L. *of table,* SANDERSON *stands* L. *of* CHUMLEY. KELLY *crosses* U.S. *and goes into* CHUMLEY'S *office* D.R. CHUMLEY *is carrying a board with papers clipped to it.*)

CHUMLEY	There is a similarity, but that Simmons woman is unco-operative, doctor. She refuses to admit to me that she has this white rabbit. Insists that it's her brother. (*Writing on board, watched by* SANDERSON.) Give her two of these at nine, another one at ten, another trip to the hydro-room at eight, and another at seven in the morning. Then we'll see if she won't co-operate tomorrow, doctor.

SANDERSON   (*Taking board*) Yes, doctor. (*He crosses to* L. *of desk and sits.*)

CHUMLEY   (*Putting pen away*) You know where to find me if you want me. Ready, pet?

BETTY   Yes, Willie – and oh, Willie –

CHUMLEY   Yes –

BETTY   There was a man in here – a man named (*Crosses to table* R.) – let me see – oh, here's his card – Dowd – Elwood P. Dowd.

             (KELLY *enters from* D.R. *with* CHUMLEY'S *hat, jacket and gloves. During the following dialogue she helps him out of his white jacket and into his suit jacket.*)

SANDERSON   That's Mrs Simmons' brother, doctor. I gave him full visiting privileges.

CHUMLEY   She can't see anyone tonight. Not anyone at all. Tell him that.

BETTY   Oh, he didn't ask to see her. He was looking for someone – some friend of his.

CHUMLEY   Oh? Who could that be, Dr Sanderson?

SANDERSON   I don't know, doctor.

BETTY   He said it was someone he came out here with this afternoon.

SANDERSON   Was there anyone with Dowd when you saw him, Miss Kelly?

KELLY — (*Giving hat to* CHUMLEY) No, doctor, not when I saw him.

BETTY — Well, he said there was. He said he last saw his friend sitting here with his hat and coat. He seemed quite disappointed.

KELLY — (*A strange look is crossing her face*) Dr Sanderson!

BETTY — I told him if we located his friend we'd give him a lift into town. He could ride in the back seat. Is that all right, Willie?

CHUMLEY — (*Moving* U.S. *towards doors*) Of course – of course.

BETTY — Oh, here it is. I wrote it down on the back. (*Showing card.*) His friend's name was Harvey.

KELLY — Harvey!

BETTY — He didn't give me the last name. He mentioned something else about him – pooka – but I didn't quite get what that was.

SANDERSON and CHUMLEY — Harvey!

(SANDERSON *rises.* CHUMLEY *has turned and is moving* D.S. *towards* BETTY *with a peculiar set look.*)

BETTY — He said his friend was very tall – and he said his friend was very ... (*She breaks off and backs* D.S.R. *as* CHUMLEY *slowly continues his advance. Alarmed.*) Why are you looking like that, Willie? He was a nice polite man and he merely asked if we could ...

CHUMLEY — (*Throwing his own hat on to table*) Get me that hat!

(KELLY *runs off* U.L. *to get hat.*)

SANDERSON   Where did he go, Mrs Chumley? How long
                 ago was he here?

BETTY   Oh – just a few minutes ago.

                 (CHUMLEY *rushes across to* R. *of desk and searches
                 rapidly through a small pocket notebook.*
                 SANDERSON *sits* L. *of desk and operates
                 dictaphone.* BETTY *walks* R. *of table* U.S. *to
                 window.*)

SANDERSON   Henry!

MALE VOICE   Main Gate.

SANDERSON   Have you seen a little man in a brown coat
                 and bow-tie leave the grounds?

MALE VOICE   A little man in a brown coat and bow-tie? Oh
                 yes, doctor; he went out a few minutes ago.

SANDERSON   You mean he's gone?

MALE VOICE   Yes, doctor.

                 (*During the dictaphone conversation* CHUMLEY
                 *has been dialling rapidly on the telephone. He now
                 breaks in.*)

CHUMLEY   (*Into phone*) Judge Gaffney? This is Dr
                 William Chumley, the psychiatrist, speaking,
                 judge. You telephoned out here this
                 afternoon about having a client of yours
                 committed. How do you spell that name?
                 With a "w" – not a "u"? Mr Elwood P. Dowd.
                 Thank you, judge. thank you very much.

                 (SANDERSON *buries his face in his hands. Chumley
                 bangs down the phone, slaps one hand on the desk,
                 then rises and bangs his hands together behind his
                 back.* KELLY *has come in with the hat and is
                 standing behind* CHUMLEY. *She jumps as he bangs
                 his hands.*)

CHUMLEY   (*To* SANDERSON) Dr Sanderson. Your name is Sanderson, I believe?

(SANDERSON *rises.*)

You specialise in the study of psychiatry? Perhaps they forgot to tell you that a rabbit has large pointed ears – that a hat for a rabbit (*taking hat from* KELLY) would have to be perforated to make room for those ears? (*He pushes two fingers through the holes in the hat, towards* SANDERSON.)

SANDERSON   Mr Dowd seemed perfectly reasonable this afternoon, doctor.

CHUMLEY   (*Throwing hat on desk*) Doctor! The function of a psychiatrist is to tell the difference between those who are reasonable and those who merely act and talk reasonable. (*Going to* U.S. *of desk.*) Do you realise what you have done to me? (*Presses buzzer.*) You don't answer; I'll tell you. You have allowed a psychopathic case to walk off these grounds and roam around with an overgrown white rabbit! You have subjected me – a psychiatrist – to the humiliation of having to call, of all things, a lawyer to find out who came out here to be committed and who came out here to commit.

(*Enter* WILSON, C. *He stands to* R. *of* CHUMLEY, *waiting.*)

SANDERSON   Dr Chumley – I was only trying . . .

CHUMLEY   Just a minute – please! (*To* WILSON.) Wilson, I want you. (*To* SANDERSON.) I will now have to do something I haven't done for fifteen years. I will have to go out after this patient, Elwood P. Dowd, and I will have to bring him back; and when I do bring him back your connection with this institution ends – as from that moment! (*To* WILSON.) Wilson, get the card.

(*Exit* WILSON, C.)

CHUMLEY   (*To* KELLY) Kelly, come with me and get that woman out of the tub!

(*Exit* KELLY, C.)

(*To* BETTY) Pet, tell the McClures we can't come to their cocktail party! (*Turning to door* U.C.) Never have I ...

(*He exits* C. *upstairs, muttering.*)

BETTY   (*Crossing towards* SANDERSON) Oh, now I'll have to tell the cook we'll be home for dinner! She'll be furious.

(SANDERSON *turns on his heel, picks up the notebook and exits to office* U.L.)

Wilson! Wilson!

(*Enter* WILSON, C. *with hat and coat on.*)

WILSON   Yes, ma'am.

BETTY   What's a pooka?

WILSON   A what?

BETTY   A pooka.

WILSON   You can search me, Mrs Chumley.

BETTY   (*Going to bookcase* R.) I wonder if it would be in the encyclopaedia. They have everything here. (*Takes out book and lays it on table the wrong way up. Starts to look, then leaves it.*) Oh, I daren't stop to do this now! (*Crossing* D.S.L.) Dr Chumley won't want to find me still here when he comes back. He'll raise h ... (*To* WILSON.) And we wouldn't want that, would we? (*As she exits.*) Oh dear, and I did want to go to that party. I do think it's too bad ... (*Her voice dies away in the distance.*)

(WILSON *looks after her, then goes to table and picks up encyclopaedia. Turns it the right way up with an expressive look after the departed* BETTY.)

WILSON   (*Runs forefinger under words*) P-o-o-k-a —
Pooka. From old Celtic mythology. A fairy
spirit in animal form. Always very large. The
pooka appears here and there, now and then,
to this one and that one, at his own caprice.
A wise but mis-chie-vi-ous creature. Very
found of rum-pots, crack-pots, and how are
you, Mr Wilson? (*Starts, then looks closely at
book. Slowly.*) How are you — Mr Wilson?

(*He looks up, looks round the room fearfully, then
drops the book on the table and, with a cry, runs
off* U.C.)

BLACKOUT AND CURTAIN

END OF ACT 1

ACT TWO

Scene 1

Time: *About an hour after the Curtain of Act I.*

Set: *The Dowd library. As in Act I, Scene 1.*

At Rise: Myrtle *is looking off* l.c. *Doors* r. *are closed.*

Myrtle   (*Calling*) Yes. That's right. The stairs at the
              end of the hall. Go right up. I'll be with you
              in a minute.

              (Judge Omar Gaffney *enters* r., *an elderly
              white-haired man. He looks displeased.*)

Judge   Well—where is she?

Myrtle   Where's who? Whom do you mean, Judge
              Gaffney? Sit down, won't you?

Judge   I mean your mother. Where's Veta Louise?
              (*Shuts door.*)

Myrtle   Why Judge Gaffney, you know where she is!
              She went over to the sanatorium to put
              Uncle Elwood in.

Judge   I know that. (*Crossing to table* l.) But why was
              I called at the club with a lot of hysteria?
              Couldn't even get what she was talking about.
              Carrying on something fierce. (*Pours himself a
              drink.*)

Myrtle   Mother carrying on? What about?

Judge   I don't know. She was hysterical.

Myrtle   That's strange. She took Uncle Elwood out to
              the sanatorium. All she had to do was put
              him in.

              (Judge *gulps at the whisky.* Myrtle *goes to door*
              l.c., *opens it and calls off.*)

              Can you find your way up there?

Male Voice   (*Off*) Yes, thank you, miss.

              (*She closes the door and turns to* Judge.)

MYRTLE	They found it!
JUDGE	Who? Found what? What are you talking about? (*Crossing to* R.C.)

(MYRTLE *comes* D.S. *to* L. *of* JUDGE.)

MYRTLE	Well, when Mother left the house with Uncle Elwood I went over to the real estate office to put the house on the market. And what do you think I found there?
JUDGE	Well, I don't know. I'm not a quizz-kid!
MYRTLE	Well, I found the man who was looking for a house just like this to cut up into service flats. He's going through it now.
JUDGE	Now look here, Myrtle, this house doesn't belong to you – it belongs to your Uncle Elwood.
MYRTLE	But now that Uncle Elwood's locked up Mother controls the property, doesn't she?
JUDGE	(*Suddenly flaring up and flinging his arms in the air*) Where is your mother? Where's Veta Louise? (*Crosses above table to back of chair* R. *of table.*)
MYRTLE	Judge, she went out to Chumley's Rest to tell them about Harvey and put Uncle Elwood in.
JUDGE	Then why did she call me at the club – when I was in the middle of a game ...
MYRTLE	I don't know.
JUDGE	... and scream at me to meet her here about something important? (*Sits chair* R. *of table.*)
MYRTLE	I simply don't know. Judge, have you got the deeds to this house?
JUDGE	I've got them in my safe. Myrtle, I feel pretty bad about this business of locking Elwood up.

MYRTLE	(*Out to front, disregarding* JUDGE) Mother and I will be able to take a long trip now. ...
JUDGE	Pretty bad.
MYRTLE	... out to Pasadena.
JUDGE	I always liked that boy. He could have been anything, done anything. He could have made a place for himself in the community.
MYRTLE	(*To* JUDGE) And all he did was get a big white rabbit.
JUDGE	Yes, yes – he had everything. Brains, personality, friends. Men liked him, women liked him. I liked him.
MYRTLE	(*Sits chair* L. *of table*) Are you telling me that once Uncle Elwood was like other men – that women actually liked him – I mean, in that way?
JUDGE	Oh, not since he started running around with that rabbit. But they did once. At one time that mailbox of your grandmother's was full of little blue scented envelopes for Elwood.
MYRTLE	I can't believe it.
JUDGE	Always something different about the boy.
MYRTLE	I don't doubt that.
JUDGE	Yes – he was always so calm about sudden changes in his plans. I used to admire it. I should have been suspicious. Take your average man – looking up and seeing a big white rabbit. He'd do something about it. But not Elwood. He took that calmly too. And look where it got him.
MYRTLE	You don't dream how far overboard he's gone on this white rabbit.
JUDGE	Oh yes I do. He's had that rabbit in my office many's the time. I'm old – but I don't miss much.

(*A banging is heard off* L.)

What's that noise?

MYRTLE   The prospective buyer on the third floor.

(*The door* L.C. *opens and* VETA *staggers in, her clothing crumpled and disarranged, her hat crooked and knocked about. Her arms are in the sleeves of her coat, but the coat itself is hanging down at her back. She manages to carry her handbag. She stands there helplessly.*)

MYRTLE   (*Jumps up*) Mother!

JUDGE   (*Rising*) Veta Louise! What's wrong, girl?

VETA   I never thought I'd see either of you again.

(MYRTLE *and* JUDGE *rush to* VETA *and lead her to chair* L. *of table.*)

MYRTLE   Take hold of her, Judge. She looks like she's going to faint.

VETA   Let me sit down somewhere.

JUDGE   Don't rush her, Myrtle. Take it easy, girl.

(*In some confusion they get her into the chair.*)

Get her some tea, Myrtle. (*Shouts.*) Do you want some tea, Veta?

MYRTLE   I'll get you some tea, mother. Get her coat off, Judge.

JUDGE   Let Myrtle get your coat off, Veta. Get her coat off, Myrtle.

VETA   Let me sit here ...

MYRTLE   Let her get her breath, Judge.

JUDGE   Let her get her breath.

(*Between the pair of them they get* VETA *into a worse state than ever.*)

VETA	Let me sit here a minute – and then let me get upstairs to my own bed, where I can let go.
MYRTLE	(*Kneeling* L. *of* VETA) What happened to you, mother?
VETA	Omar, I want you to sue them. They put me in and let Elwood go!
JUDGE	(*Moving round table to* R.) What's this?
MYRTLE	But why? What did you say? What did you do? You must have done something.
VETA	I didn't do one thing! I simply told them about Elwood and Harvey.
JUDGE	Then how could this happen to you? I don't understand it! (*Sits chair* R.)
VETA	I told them about Elwood and then I went down to the taxi-cab to get his things. As I was walking along the path this awful man stepped out. He was a white slaver – I know he was. He had on one of those white suits – that's how they advertise.
MYRTLE	A man! What did he do, mother?
VETA	What did he do? He took hold of me and then he took me in there, and then he ... (*She groans and buries her face in her hands.*)
JUDGE	Go on, Veta Louise. Go on, girl.
MYRTLE	Poor mother! Was he a young man?
JUDGE	Myrtle Mae – perhaps you'd better leave the room.
MYRTLE	What, now? I should say not. (*Greatly excited.*) Go on, mother!
JUDGE	What did he do, Veta?
VETA	He took me upstairs and then he tore my clothes off.

MYRTLE	Did you hear that, Judge? (*Excitedly.*) Go on, mother!
VETA	(*Giving* MYRTLE *on old-fashioned look*) And then he sat me down in a tub of water!
MYRTLE	Oh, for Heaven's sake!
VETA	I always thought what you were showed on your face. Don't you believe it, Judge. Don't you believe it, Myrtle. That man took hold of me as if I were a woman of the streets – but I fought. I always said that if a man jumped at me I'd fight. Haven't I always said that, Myrtle?
MYRTLE	Oh yes, Judge. That's what Mother always told me to do.
VETA	And then he hustled me into that sanatorium and set me down in that tub of water and began treating me as if I were a ...
MYRTLE	A what?
VETA	A crazy woman. But he did that just for spite.
JUDGE	We'll I'll be dammed.
VETA	And then those doctors came upstairs and asked me a lot of questions; all about sex-urges and all that filthy stuff. That place ought to be cleaned up, Omar. You'd better get the authorities to clean it up. Myrtle, don't you ever go out there! Do you hear me?
JUDGE	(*Rises*) This stinks to high heaven, Veta; my God it does!
VETA	You've go to do something about it, Judge. You've got to sue them.
JUDGE	I will. My God I will. (*Crosses below table to* L.C.) If Chumley thinks he can run an unsavoury place like this on the outskirts of town, he'll be publicly chastised. I'll run him out of the town.

VETA   Tell me, Judge; is that all those doctors do in
            places like that – think about sex?

JUDGE   (*Crosses back above table to* R. *and leaning on
            back of chair* R. *of table*) I don't know.

VETA   Because, if it is, they ought to be ashamed of
            themselves. It's all in their hands, anyway.
            Why don't they get out and go for long walks
            in the country?

JUDGE   Exactly! Exactly! (*Crosses to* L.)

VETA   (*As* JUDGE *is crossing*) Judge Gaffney walked
            everywhere for years –

            (JUDGE *stops dead.*)

            – didn't you, Judge?

JUDGE   (*Crosses below table to chair* R. *and sitting*) Now,
            let me take some notes on this. (*Produces small
            notebook and pencil.*) You say these two doctors
            came up to talk to you – Dr Chumley and –
            what was the other doctor's name?

VETA   Sanderson. But, Judge, don't pay any
            attention to anything he tells you. He's a liar.
            Close-set-eyes – they're always liars. Besides –
            I told him something in the strictest
            confidence – and he blabbed it.

MYRTLE   What did you tell him, mother?

VETA   Never you mind. Let's forget it. I don't even
            want to talk about it. (*She rises.*) You can't
            trust anybody.

JUDGE   Anything you said to Dr Sanderson you can
            tell us. This is your daughter. I am your
            lawyer.

VETA   Well, I know which is which! I don't want to
            talk about it. I want you to sue them, and I
            want to get upstairs to my own bed.

            (JUDGE *and* MYRTLE *rise.*)

MYRTLE	But, mother – this is the important thing, anyway. Where is Uncle Elwood?
VETA	I should have known better than to try to do anything about him. Something protects him – that awful pooka!
MYRTLE	Mother, please answer me! Where is Uncle Elwood?
VETA	How should I know? They let him go! They're not interested in men in places like that. You know that, Myrtle. Don't be so naive!
	(*Noise is heard, off* L.)
	What's that noise?
MYRTLE	I've found a buyer for the house.
VETA	What?
MYRTLE	Look, mother, we've got to find Uncle Elwood. No matter who jumped at you, we've still got to lock up Uncle Elwood.
VETA	I don't know where he is. The next time, you take him, Judge. (*Goes* U.S. *to door* L.C.) You wait till Elwood hears what they did to me. He won't stand for it. Don't forget to sue them, Judge. Myrtle Mae, all I hope is that never, never as long as you live (*hysterical and almost in tears*) a man pulls the clothes off you and sits you down in a tub of water! (*Exits* L.C.)
MYRTLE	(*At* L.C.) Now see – Mother's muffed everything. No matter what happened out there. Uncle Elwood is still wandering around with Harvey.
JUDGE	(*He's pondering*) The thing for me to do is to take some more notes.
MYRTLE	It's all Uncle Elwood's fault. He found out what she was up to and had her put in. Then he ran.

JUDGE   (*Crossing to* MYRTLE) Now, don't say that.
                Your Uncle Elwood thinks the world of your
                mother. Ever since he was a little boy he
                always wanted to share everything he had
                with her.

MYRTLE   I'm not giving up. We'll get detectives. We'll
                find him. And, besides, you'd better save
                some of that sympathy for me and mother.
                You don't realise what we have to put up
                with. Wait till I show you something he
                brought home about six months ago, and we
                hid it out in the garage. You just wait, Judge.

                (*Exits* L.C.)

JUDGE   Yes, yes. She knows more than she's telling. I
                sense that. (*Sits* L. *of table, writing in notebook.*)
                Sanderson. S-A-N-D-E . . .

                (WILSON, *wearing overcoat and carrying hat,
                rushes in from* D.R.)

WILSON   (*Crossing to above table and leaning over it
                towards* JUDGE) O.K. Is he here?

JUDGE   (*Looking up, startled*) What's that?

WILSON   The crackpot with the rabbit. Is he here?

JUDGE   No.

                (WILSON *turns and rushes out again* R.)

                And who, may I ask, are you?

WILSON   (*Calling, off* R.) Not here, doctor.

CHUMLEY   (*Off* R.) I'm coming up.

WILSON   (*Returning to* R. *of* JUDGE) Dr Chumley's
                coming up. What's your name?

JUDGE   Chumley? (*Slapping hand on table and rising.*)
                Well, well. (*Crossing to* L.) I've something to
                say to him.

WILSON	(*Following him*) What's your name? Let's have it!
JUDGE	I am Judge Gaffney. Where is Dr Chumley?
WILSON	The reason I ask is – the doctor always likes to know who he's talking to.
	(*Enter* CHUMLEY D.R.) This guy says his name's Judge Gaffney, doctor.
JUDGE	Well, Chumley ...
CHUMLEY	Good evening, Judge. Let's not waste time. (*Crosses to* R.C.) Has he been here?
JUDGE	Elwood? – no. But see here, doctor ... (*Crosses towards* CHUMLEY, *but* WILSON *steps between them, facing* CHUMLEY.)
WILSON	Sure he ain't been here. He's wise now – he's hiding. (*Crosses to doors* R. *and closing them.*) It'll be a 'ell of a job to smoke him out.
CHUMLEY	(*Puts hat and gloves on table and sits chair* L. *of table*) It will be more difficult. They're sly – they're cunning. But I get them. I always get them. Wilson, have you the list of places we've been to? (*To* JUDGE, *indicating* WILSON.) My attendant, Marvin Wilson.
WILSON	(*At* C.) We've been to seventeen bars. Eddie's place, Charlie's place, Bessie's Barndance, the Old Beadly Buddly Bo, the New Beadly Buddly Bo, and the Beadly Buddly Bo Annexe across the street. The Union Station, the city incinerator ... (*To* JUDGE.) Say, why does a guy like this go down to the city incinerator?
JUDGE	Because the foreman is a friend of his. He has many friends, in many places.
CHUMLEY	(*Toying unconcernedly with his gloves on the table*) I have called here to ask Mrs Simmons if she has any other suggestions as to where we might look for him.

JUDGE   (*Sternly*) Dr Chumley!

CHUMLEY   (*Turning his head slowly towards* JUDGE, *very
                 much master of the situation*) H'm?

JUDGE   (*Going up to* CHUMLEY) It is my solemn duty
                 to inform you that Mrs Simmons has retained
                 me to file a suit against you for what
                 happened to her in your sanatorium this
                 afternoon.

CHUMLEY   (*Rising and standing face to face with* JUDGE) A
                 suit!

JUDGE   And while we're . .

WILSON   (*Closing in behind* JUDGE, *so that he is tightly
                 sandwiched between* WILSON *and* CHUMLEY)
                 That's pretty, ain't it, doctor? After us
                 draggin' your tail all over town trying to find
                 that guy . . .

JUDGE   (*Turning and stamping on* WILSON'S *foot*) Be
                 off! Be off!

                 (WILSON *breaks* U.S. *holding his foot.*)

                 What happened this afternoon . . .

CHUMLEY   Judge Gaffney, this afternoon was an
                 unfortunate mistake. I have discharged my
                 assistant who made it – and I am willing to
                 undertake this man's case personally. It
                 interests me, and my interest in a case is
                 something no amount of money can buy.

JUDGE   But this business this afternoon, doctor . . .

CHUMLEY   (*Holding up his hand*) Water – under the dam.

                 (MYRTLE *enters* U.S.L., *carrying a big flat parcel
                 wrapped in brown paper. She places it on chair
                 just inside door and listens.*)

                 (*Breaking* D.S.R.) The important thing now is
                 to get this man and take him out to the
                 sanatorium where he belongs.

MYRTLE	(*Moving* D.S. *to* L.C.) That's right, Judge, that's just what I think.
JUDGE	Myrtle Mae, will you not ...
CHUMLEY	Excuse me, I have not had the pleasure ...
JUDGE	Oh, let me introduce – Miss Myrtle Mae Simmons, Mr Dowd's niece, Mrs Simmons' daughter.
MYRTLE	How do you do, Dr Chumley?
CHUMLEY	How do you do, Miss Simmons?
WILSON	Hullo, Myrtle!
MYRTLE	(*Now seeing him and staring at him with a mixture of horror and curiosity*) What? Oh ...
CHUMLEY	And now may I speak to Mrs Simmons?
MYRTLE	Mother won't come down, doctor. I just know she won't. (*To* JUDGE.) You try to get Mother to talk to him, Judge.
JUDGE	Now, see here: Veta Louise was manhandled. She was ... she was ... was ... God knows what she was. This man's approach to her was not professional; it was personal. (*He looks at* WILSON.)
CHUMLEY	Wilson, this is a serious charge.
WILSON	Dr Chumley – I've been with you ten years. (*Closing on* JUDGE.) Are you going to believe this ... (*To* JUDGE.) What's your name again?
JUDGE	Gaffney. Judge Omar Gaffney.
WILSON	Thanks. (*To* CHUMLEY.) You're goin' to believe this old geezer Gaffney? ...
CHUMLEY	Wilson!
WILSON	Me! Me and a dame what sees a rabbit!
JUDGE	It is not Mrs Simmons who sees the rabbit. It's her brother.

MYRTLE	Yes, it's Uncle Elwood.
JUDGE	(*Crossing to door* U.L.C.) If you'll come with me, doctor.
CHUMLEY	(*Crossing to door* U.L.C.) Very well, Judge.
	(JUDGE *exits.*)
	(*In doorway.*) Wilson, I have a situation here. Wait for me. (*Exits.*)
WILSON	O.K., doctor.
	(MYRTLE *is left standing* L.C. WILSON *comes shyly towards her.*)
	So your name's Myrtle Mae?
MYRTLE	Yes.
WILSON	If we grab your uncle, you're liable to be comin' out to the sanatorium on visiting days?
MYRTLE	Well, I don't really know. I ...
WILSON	Because if you are – I'll be there!
MYRTLE	Oh, will you?
WILSON	And if you don't see me right away – don't give up. Stick around – I'll show up.
MYRTLE	Oh, will you? (*Getting interested.*)
WILSON	Sure! You heard Dr Chumley tell me to wait?
MYRTLE	Yes.
WILSON	Tell you what –
	(*They get closer to each other.*)
MYRTLE	What?
WILSON	While I'm waiting –
MYRTLE	Yes?
WILSON	There's something I wish you'd give me –
MYRTLE	Oh, what? (*Very excited.*)

WILSON	A ham sandwich and a glass of milk.
MYRTLE	(*Thoroughly let down*) Oh, well – the kitchen's through here. (*Going* U.S. *to door.*)
WILSON	(*Following her*) Yes, sir! You're all right, Myrtle. You're O.K.
	(MYRTLE *is in the doorway* U.L.C., WILSON *is to* R. *of her, facing.*)
	Tell you something else, Myrtle, on the level –
MYRTLE	What?
WILSON	You've not only got a nice build – but you've got something else too –
MYRTLE	(*Close to him and quite excited*) Oh, what?
WILSON	You've got the screwiest uncle that ever stuck his nose inside our nuthouse!
	(MYRTLE *turns away in disgust and exits, followed by* WILSON. *The stage is empty. From* R. *enters* ELWOOD, *singing. He carries a piece of paper on which is written a telephone number. He is wearing has hat.*)
ELWOOD	(*Singing*) I'm sitting on top of the world. Rolling along . . . (*He has reached the telephone. Still singing.*) All alone on the telephone. (*On one note.*) We will get a little three (*dials three, rather unsteadily*) and a little five. (*Dials five.*) One, two, three, four, five. And another little three wouldn't do us any harm. (*Stands upright, holding receiver and listening. Apparently nothing happens. He looks disgustedly at the receiver and shakes it. Then peers at his piece of paper, laid on the table.*) Another little five! (*Dials it, then listens again. While waiting he sings.*) First you hop on your little left shoe; then you hop on the other one too; that's the Hopscotch – (*He breaks off.*) – Scotch! (*He looks at the decanter of whisky and solemnly raises*

*his hat to it. Then, apparently, someone answers
the phone.*) Hullo! Is that Chumley's Rest? Is
Dr Chumley there? Oh, that's Mrs Chumley!
(*Raises hat.*) This is Elwood P. Dowd speaking.
How are you this evening? That's good. Tell
me, Mrs C, were you able to locate Harvey?
Oh, don't worry – I'll find him. I'm just back
from McClure's cocktail party! I met some
nice people there and I was able to leave
quite a few of my cards. Well, I waited till
you phoned to say you couldn't come because
some patient had escaped. Where am I? I'm
here! But I must go now – I must find
Harvey. Good-bye, Mrs Chumley (*Raises hat.*)
– my regards to you and anybody else you
happen to run into. Good night, my dear.
(*Replaces phone. Singing.*) Good night, my
dear. (*He moves* U.S.C. *and catches sight of the
parcel on the chair. He breaks off.*) Oh, so you've
turned up. Let's have a look at you. (*Unties
string and puts it in his pocket, singing.*) Just a
little bit of string. (*Removes paper.*) Wonderful
– how do you look in the light? (*Holds up
picture, his back to audience. We see an oil-
painting of* ELWOOD *seated, behind him and
looking over his shoulder a large white rabbit.*)
Wonderful! Now, where shall we put you?
Somewhere very conspicious – very
conspicious. (*Looks round room, then sees picture
over mantelpiece.*) That's the place! (*Takes
picture over and sets it in front of picture of Mrs
Dowd so that it covers it completely. He steps back
to admire it and treads on the paper lying on the
floor. During the following monologue he folds up
the paper methodically.*)

Let's be tidy!
Let's be house-proud!
Can't have bits of paper lying about the
house: no!
Mustn't make a litter! – A litter!

(*As he says "a litter" he looks over to the picture, raises his hat, then exits* R., *laughing, the folded paper under his arm.* VETA *enters* U.L.C. *wearing an elaborate négligé; she is followed by* CHUMLEY.)

VETA   Doctor, you might just as well go home and wait. I'm suing you for fifty thousand dollars, and that's final.

(*Telephone rings.* VETA *goes to answer it. She has not looked at the mantelpiece.*)

CHUMLEY   (*At* C., *turning and seeing picture*) Mrs Simmons!

VETA   (*To* CHUMLEY) Yes, doctor?

CHUMLEY   That picture over your mantel!

VETA   That portrait, doctor, happens to be the pride of this house! (*To phone.*) Yes?

CHUMLEY   Well – who painted it?

VETA   (*To* CHUMLEY) Who painted it? Oh, some man. He was around for the sittings; we paid him and he went away. (*To phone.*) Hullo! Yes? No – this is Dexter 1567. (*Hangs up.*)

CHUMLEY   Well, I suppose if you have money enough to pay people, you can persuade them to do anything.

VETA   Dr Chumley (*she walks over to him*), you brought this up; you may as well learn something. I took a course in art this last winter. The difference between a fine oil-painting and a mechanical thing like a photograph is simply this: A photograph shows only the reality. A painting shows not only the reality but the dream behind it! It's our dreams that keep us going. (*Crosses below table to* R.C.) I wouldn't want to live if I thought it was all just eating and sleeping and taking off my clothes – I mean

	(*remembering her unfortunate experience*) putting them on again! (*Turning, she sees the picture, screams, totters and falls back on to chair* L. *of table*.) Oh! Oh! Doctor!
CHUMLEY	(*Taking her hand*) Steady now – don't get excited. Everything's all right.
VETA	(*Pointing to picture*) Doctor, that is not my mother!
CHUMLEY	I'm glad to hear that.
VETA	Doctor, Elwood's been here. He's been here.
	(*Telephone rings.*)
CHUMLEY	Don't worry; don't worry. I'll answer it for you. (*He answers it.*) Hello? Yes? (*Drops his hand over mouthpiece.*) Here he is! Mrs Simmons, your brother.
VETA	(*Rising*) Oh – let me talk to him.
CHUMLEY	(*Hands phone to* VETA. *He crosses to* R.C.) Don't tell him I'm here. Be casual.
VETA	(*To phone*) Hullo, Elwood! Where are you? What? Oh, just a minute (*Covers phone.*) He won't say where he is. He wants to know if Harvey is here.
CHUMLEY	Tell him – Harvey is here.
VETA	(*Too quickly*) But he isn't!
CHUMLEY	Well – tell him. That way we'll find out where he is. Humour him – we have to humour them.
VETA	(*To phone*) Yes, Elwood, Harvey is here. Why don't you come home? (*Covers phone.*) It won't work. He says I'm to call Harvey to the telephone.
CHUMLEY	(*Decisively*) Tell him Harvey is here but he can't come to the telephone.
VETA	Why not?

CHUMLEY	Well – say he's in the bath.
VETA	(*Lifts phone to speak and then lowers it*) Oh, doctor!
CHUMLEY	We've got to do it.
VETA	(*To phone, resignedly*) Yes, Elwood, Harvey is here, but he's in the bath. I'll send him over as soon as he's dry. Where are you? Elwood! Elwood! (*Bangs and shakes phone.*)
CHUMLEY	Did he ring off?
VETA	Harvey – just walked in at the door! He says I'm to look in the bath – it must be a stranger! But I know where he is – I heard the barman answer the other telephone; he's at Charlie's place. That's a bar over at Twelfth and Main.
CHUMLEY	Twelfth and Main. That's two blocks down and one over, isn't it? (*Picks up hat from table and is reaching for gloves when* VETA *stops him.*)
VETA	Doctor! Where are you going?
CHUMLEY	(*Coming back to* C.) I'm going over there to get your brother and take him out to the sanatorium where he belongs.
VETA	Oh, doctor – don't do that! Send one of your attendants. I'm warning you.
CHUMLEY	But, Mrs Simmons, if I'm to help your brother ...
VETA	He can't be helped. There's no help for him. He's got to be picked up and blocked up and left.
CHUMLEY	You consider your brother a dangerous man?
VETA	Dangerous!
CHUMLEY	Why?
VETA	Well, I won't tell you why – but if I didn't, why would I want him locked up?

CHUMLEY   Then I must observe this man. I must watch
            the expression on his face as he talks to the
            rabbit. He does talk to the rabbit, you say?

VETA   Oh – they tell each other everything!

CHUMLEY   What's that?

VETA   I said – "Of course he talks to him." But
            don't go, doctor. You'll regret it if you do.

CHUMLEY   (*Going above table to* R. *and picking up gloves*)
            Nonsense, Mrs Simmons! You underestimate
            me.

VETA   Oh no, doctor – you underestimate my
            brother!

CHUMLEY   (*Putting on his hat*) Not at all. Don't worry
            now. I can handle him. (*He pats the top of his
            hat confidently and exits* R., *closing the doors
            behind him.*)

VETA   (*After he has gone*) You can handle him? That's
            all you think? (*A sudden thought strikes her. She
            goes to door* U.L.C. *and opens it. Calling off.*)
            Myrtle Mae! Myrtle Mae – just go and see
            who's in the bath! (*Turns to front, realising
            what she has said.*)

            ⟡ BLACKOUT AND CURTAIN

            END OF SCENE 1

                         SCENE 2

TIME: *Four hours after the Curtain of Scene 1.*

SET: *The office at Chumley's Rest. As in Act I, Scene 2,
            except that the bracket fittings on the walls are
            alight and the curtains are drawn. All doors are
            closed.*

AT RISE: KELLY *is seated at* L. *of desk, on the telephone.*

KELLY   (*To phone*) Thank you, sergeant. I may call
            later. (*Hangs up.*)

(SANDERSON *enters from* U.L., *followed by*
WILSON. *They are both carrying books and*
SANDERSON *also has a strap. He has removed his*
white jacket and is wearing a dark double-breasted
suit.)

WILSON   (*As they cross to table* R.) How about that stuff
              in your room, doctor?

SANDERSON   (*Putting books on table*) All packed, thank you,
              Wilson.

WILSON   (*Putting down books*) Tough you getting
              bounced. I had you figured for one who'd
              make the grade.

              (*During the following dialogue* SANDERSON *does*
              up his books in the strap, putting some in bookcase
              and getting others out.)

SANDERSON   Those are the breaks.

WILSON   When you takin' off?

SANDERSON   As soon as Dr Chumley gets back.

WILSON   (*Crossing to* R. *of desk, to* KELLY) Oh, Kelly, did
              you get a report back yet from the desk
              sergeant in the police accident bureau?

KELLY   Not yet. I just talked to the downtown
              dispensary. They haven't seen him.

WILSON   It's beginning to smell awful funny to me.
              Four hours he's been gone – and not a word
              from him. (*Goes to* SANDERSON, *extending*
              hand.) Oh, doctor, I may not see you again,
              so I want to say I wish you a lot of luck – and
              I'm mighty sorry you got a kick in the pants.

SANDERSON   Thanks, Wilson – good luck to you too.

WILSON   (*Starts to exit* U.C. *but stops and turns to* KELLY)
              Look, Kelly, let me know if you hear from
              the desk sergeant, will you? If there's no sign
              of the doctor I'm goin' into town to look for
              him. He ought to know better'n to go after a
              psycho without me. (*Starts* U.C.)

SANDERSON	(*Going to* WILSON) I'd like to help you look for the doctor, too, Wilson.
WILSON	That's swell of you, doctor, right after he gave you the sack.
SANDERSON	Oh – I've no resentment against Dr Chumley. He was right – I was wrong. Chumley is the biggest man in his field and it's my loss not to be able to work with him. (*Crosses back to table.*)
WILSON	You're not so small yourself, doctor.
SANDERSON	Thanks, Wilson.
WILSON	Don't mention it.
	(*Exits* U.C.)
KELLY	(*Rising and taking a deep breath*) Dr Sanderson –
SANDERSON	(*Busy with books*) Yes?
KELLY	(*Crossing to* R.C.) Well, doctor, I'd just like to say that I wish you a lot of luck too, and I'm sorry to see you leave.
SANDERSON	(*Going on with his work*) Are you sure you can spare all those good wishes, Miss Kelly?
KELLY	(*Taken aback*) On second thoughts, I don't suppose I can. (*Turns back to below desk.*) Forget it!
SANDERSON	(*Looking up*) Miss Kelly, this is for nothing – just a little advice. I'd be awfully careful, if I were you, about the kind of company I kept.
KELLY	I beg your pardon, doctor!
SANDERSON	(*Crosses to* C.) Saturday night at the Frontier Hotel, dancing with that – that . . .
KELLY	Oh, did you? I didn't notice you!
SANDERSON	I'd be a little careful of him, Kelly. He looked to me like a schizophrenic (*Turning back to table.*) – all the way across the floor.

(*There are a few books lying on the desk.* KELLY
picks one up and carries it across to SANDERSON.)

KELLY   You really shouldn't have given him a
                   thought, doctor. (*Hands him the book.*) He was
                   my date – not yours.

SANDERSON   That was his mentality. The rest of him –
                   well . . .

KELLY   (*Crossing back slowly towards desk*) She was
                   beautiful though.

SANDERSON   Who?

KELLY   That girl you were with.

SANDERSON   Oh – I thought you didn't notice.

KELLY   (*Scoring a point as she goes back to* L. *of desk*)
                   You bumped into us twice – how could I
                   help it?

SANDERSON   (*Getting annoyed*) Not that it makes any
                   difference to you – but that girl happens to
                   be a very charming little lady. *She* has a
                   sweet, kind disposition – and *she* knows how
                   to behave herself!

                   (KELLY *has picked up a book and is pretending to
                   read it. She looks up at him over the top of the
                   book as she scores again.*)

KELLY   (*Sweetly sarcastic*) Funny she couldn't get a
                   better date – on a Saturday night.

SANDERSON   And she has an excellent mind.

KELLY   Why doesn't she use it?

SANDERSON   (*He has strapped up his books now, and puts the
                   pile down rather firmly on the table. Crosses to* R.
                   of desk, facing KELLY *across it*) Oh, I don't
                   suppose you're to be blamed for the flippant,
                   hard shell you have. You're probably
                   compensating for something.

KELLY   I am not – and don't you try any of your (*she prods him with the book*) psychiatry on me. (*She puts down the book and turns away from him, folding arms.*)

SANDERSON   (*Picking up ruler*) Oh, if I could only try something else on you – just once! (*Raising ruler as if to strike her.*) Just once – just to see if you'd melt under any circumstances. (*Raises ruler again.*) No, I doubt it.

KELLY   (*Turning*) You'll never know, doctor.

SANDERSON   Because you interest me – as a case-history, that's all. I'd like to know where you get that inflated ego.

KELLY   (*Now close to tears*) Oh! – if you aren't the meanest person. (*Crossing below desk and turning* U.C.) Inflated ego!

    (*Telephone rings.*)

    Case-history!

    (KELLY *goes to doorway* U.C.)

SANDERSON   (*Turning to* U.S.) Don't run away! Let's finish it.

KELLY   Oh, leave me alone!

SANDERSON   All right. (*Shrugging his shoulders, he exits* U.L. *to office.*)

    (*The telephone is still ringing.* KELLY *looks after him for a moment, then answers phone.*)

KELLY   (*Very crossly*) Chumley's Rest! (*Changes tone.*) Oh yes, sergeant; no accident report on him in town or suburbs.

    (ELWOOD *enters* D.L., *carrying bunch of dahlias.*)

    (*Seeing* ELWOOD.) Oh, it's all right, sergeant. (*Hangs up. To* ELWOOD.) Mr Dowd!

ELWOOD   Miss Kelly! These flowers are for you. (*Hands flowers and crosses to* R.C.)

KELLY	(*Taking flowers*) For me? Oh, thank you!
ELWOOD	You'll find they're quite fresh – I just picked them outside.
KELLY	(*Horror-struck*) I only hope Dr Chumley didn't see you – they're his prize dahlias! Did Dr Chumley go upstairs?
ELWOOD	Not knowing, I cannot state. Those flowers look lovely against your hair.
KELLY	I've never worn orange before – it's such a trying colour.
ELWOOD	You would improve any colour, my dear.
KELLY	Thank you!
ELWOOD	Not at all.
KELLY	Did – did Dr Chumley go over to his house?
ELWOOD	I don't know. Where is Dr Sanderson?
KELLY	In his office here, I think.
SANDERSON	(*Entering* U.L.) Miss Kelly! (*Sees* DOWD.) Dowd! – there you are!
ELWOOD	I have a cab outside if it's possible for you and Miss Kelly to get away now.
SANDERSON	(*Coming to* C.) Where's Dr Chumley?
ELWOOD	Is he coming too? Splendid!
	(KELLY *signals "I don't know".*)
	I must apologise for being a little late. I thought Miss Kelly should have some flowers. After what happened out here this afternoon, doctor, these flowers should really have come from you. (*Putting hand on* SANDERSON'S *shoulder.*) Ah, my boy – as you grow older and pretty women pass you by, you will think with deep gratitude of these generous girls of your youth. Shall we be going?
SANDERSON	Just a minute, Dowd.

ELWOOD   As you say. (*Places hat on table* R.)

                (SANDERSON *signals to* KELLY *to fetch* WILSON.
                She exits U.C.)

SANDERSON   Mr Dowd, the situation has changed
                considerably since this afternoon. But I urge
                you to bear no resentment. Dr Chumley is
                your friend. He only wants to help you.

ELWOOD   That's kind of him. All I want is to help him
                too.

SANDERSON   If you'll begin by taking a co-operative
                attitude, that's half the battle. We all have to
                face reality, Dowd, sooner or later.

ELWOOD   Reality! I wrestled with reality for forty years,
                doctor, and I am happy to state that I've now
                got reality just where I want it!

                (*Enter* WILSON, C., *followed by* KELLY.)

WILSON   There you are! (*Goes over to* ELWOOD.)
                Upstairs, buddy! We're going upstairs. Is the
                doctor O.K.?

ELWOOD   There must be some mistake. Miss Kelly and
                Dr Sanderson and I are going over to
                Charlie's place. I'd be very happy if you come
                with us, Mr Wilson. They have a floor show.

WILSON   Yeah? Well, wait till you see the floor show
                we've got! Upstairs, buddy! (*He grabs* ELWOOD
                by the arm and takes him up to doorway C.)

SANDERSON   Just a minute, Wilson. Mr Dowd – where did
                you say Dr Chumley went?

ELWOOD   (*Moving down*) As I said before – he didn't
                confide his plans to me.

WILSON   You mean the doctor ain't showed up yet?

KELLY   Not yet.

WILSON   Where is he?

SANDERSON   That's what we're trying to find out.

KELLY	Mr Dowd walked in here by himself, Wilson.
WILSON	Oh, he did, did he? (*Crosses to* ELWOOD, *who is standing by chair* L. *of table*.) Listen, you; talk fast or I'm working you over!
ELWOOD	Oh, I'd rather you didn't do that, Mr Wilson – and I'd rather you didn't even mention such a thing in the presence of a lovely young lady like Miss Kelly. (*Making eyes at* KELLY *behind* SANDERSON's *back*.)
SANDERSON	Mr Dowd, Dr Chumley went into town to pick you up. That was four hours ago.
ELWOOD	Oh, where has the evening gone to?
WILSON	Listen to that! Smart, eh!
SANDERSON	Just a minute, Wilson. Mr Dowd, did you see Dr Chumley tonight?
ELWOOD	Yes – he came into Charlie's place at dinner-time. Now, that's a cosy spot – let's all go over there and have a drink!
WILSON	We're going no place. (*Crosses in front of* SANDERSON, *going close up to* ELWOOD.) Now, I'm asking you a question, and if you don't button up your lip and give me some straight answers I'm goin' to beat it out of you!
ELWOOD	But what you suggest is impossible, Mr Wilson.
WILSON	(*Menacingly*) What's that?
ELWOOD	Well – you ask me to button up my lip – and give you some straight answers (*pulling* WILSON *by the ear*); it can't be done!
	(WILSON *makes to seize him*.)
SANDERSON	Wilson! Wilson! Wilson! Will you let me handle this – please?
WILSON	Well, handle it then. But find out where the doctor is (*Goes to doors* U.C. *and closes them*.)

(ELWOOD *sits chair* L. *of table, his hat on the table.* SANDERSON *goes up to him.*)

SANDERSON   Mr Dowd, you say Dr Chumley did come into Charlie's place tonight?

ELWOOD   Yes – and I was very pleased to see him.

WILSON   (*From* U.C.) Go on –

ELWOOD   Well, he asked for me, and naturally the proprieter brought him over. We exchanged the conventional greetings. I said, "Good evening, Dr Chumley." He said, "Good evening, Mr Dowd." I believe we said that at least once.

WILSON   O.K. – O.K.

ELWOOD   I'm trying to be factual. Then I introduced him to Harvey.

WILSON   To who?

KELLY   (*From* L. *of desk*) A white rabbit, six feet tall.

WILSON   (*Incredulous*) Six feet!

ELWOOD   Six feet, one and a half.

WILSON   O.K., O.K. – fool around with him; and all the time the doctor's probably some place bleedin' to death in a ditch!

ELWOOD   Well, if those were his plans for the evening, didn't tell me about it.

SANDERSON   Go on, Dowd.

ELWOOD   Well – Dr Chumley sat down at the table with us. Let's see, now – I was sitting on the outside like this – Harvey was sitting on the inside near the wall. And then Dr Chumley sat down opposite Harvey so that he could look at him.

WILSON   (*Moving a little nearer*) That's right, spend all the night on the seating arrangements!

ELWOOD	Harvey then suggested that I should buy him a drink. Well, knowing that Harvey doesn't like to drink alone, I suggested that Dr Chumley and I should join him.
WILSON	And so –
ELWOOD	We joined him.
WILSON	Then what?
ELWOOD	We joined him again.
WILSON	Then what happened?
ELWOOD	Ha-ha! We kept on joining him!
WILSON	Oh, will you skip all the joining?
ELWOOD	Well – you're asking me to skip the best part of the evening.
WILSON	Tell us what happened – please.
ELWOOD	Then the doctor and Harvey got into conversation – quietly at first. Then I'm afraid the doctor raised his voice.
WILSON	Yeah? Why?
ELWOOD	Well, Harvey seemed to feel that Dr Chumley should assume part of the financial responsibility of the joining – but the doctor didn't seem to want to do that.
KELLY	I can believe that part of it!
WILSON	Let him go on. Let's see how far he'll go. This guy's got guts!
ELWOOD	Well, I didn't want any trouble – so I decided to take the whole thing over. You see, we go down to Charlie's place quite a lot, Harvey and I. The proprietor is a fine man, with a very interesting approach to life. Then – the other matter came up.
WILSON	Will you cut the damned double-talk and get on with it!

ELWOOD   (*Rising*) Mr Wilson, you are a sincere type of
              person, but I must ask you not to use such
              language in the presence of a lovely young
              lady like Miss Kelly. (*He bends forwards and
              backwards, trying to see* KELLY *the other side of*
              SANDERSON.)

SANDERSON   You're right, sir, and we're very sorry.

ELWOOD   Ah! (*He bows elaborately to* SANDERSON.)

              (SANDERSON *bows back, claps his hand to his
              forehead, then moves* U.S.C. ELWOOD *bows
              elaborately to* KELLY, *who returns his bow. He
              then signals to* WILSON *and* KELLY *that they
              should bow to each other. They do so,* WILSON
              very stiffly, as if hypnotised. WILSON *is above desk,
              in front of doors,* KELLY *to* L. *of desk.* SANDERSON
              comes D.S.C.)

SANDERSON   Mr Dowd – You said just now, the other
              matter came up?

ELWOOD   (*Sitting*) Oh yes. There was a beautiful blonde
              woman – a Mrs Smethills – and her escort
              sitting at a table opposite to us. Then Dr
              Chumley went over to sit next to her and
              explained that they had met somewhere once
              – in Chicago. Then – her escort escorted Dr
              Chumley back to Harvey and myself and
              tried to point out that it would be better for
              the doctor if he minded his own affairs. Does
              he have any?

KELLY   Please hurry, Mr Dowd; we're all so worried.

ELWOOD   Of course. Then the doctor urged Harvey to
              go with him over to Blondie's Chicken Inn,
              but Harvey seemed to want to go over to
              Eddie's place instead. Well, while they were
              arguing about, I went over to get myself
              another drink and when I came back – they'd
              gone!

WILSON	Well, where did they go? I mean – where did the doctor go?
ELWOOD	I don't know. You see, I had a date out here with Dr Sanderson and Miss Kelly, and I came out to pick them up – hoping that during the evening we might run into Harvey and that doctor and make a party of it.
WILSON	So – you've got his story! (*Goes over to* ELWOOD, *fists clenched.*) O.K. – you're lying, and we know it!
ELWOOD	(*Rising*) Mr Wilson, I never lie.
WILSON	You've done something with the doctor, and I'm finding out what it is. (*He is about to seize hold of* ELWOOD.)
SANDERSON	Wilson! Wilson! Wilson!
KELLY	Maybe he isn't lying, Wilson.
WILSON	(*Breaking* U.S.L.) That's all this guy is – a bunch of lies. You don't believe this story about the doctor sitting talking to a big rabbit, do you?
KELLY	Maybe Dr Chumley did go over to Charlie's place.
WILSON	And saw a big white rabbit, I suppose?
ELWOOD	And why not? (*Sits.*) Harvey was there! At first the doctor seemed a little frightened of Harvey – but it turned to admiration as the evening wore on. As the evening wore on. That is a nice expression – with your permission I will say it again. As the evening wore on.
WILSON	(*Rushing at him*) And with your permission I'll be knocking your teeth down your throat!

ELWOOD   (*Not moving an inch*) Mr Wilson – haven't you
                  some old friends you can go away and play
                  with?

                  (WILSON *towers over him, almost bursting with
                  rage.* SANDERSON *grabs* WILSON *and pushes him
                  U.S. above table.* KELLY *looks up number in
                  telephone directory and begins dialling.*)

                  (*Rising and picking up his hat, crossing towards
                  desk.*) Well, this is all very stimulating, but I
                  really must be going.

KELLY   (*On phone*) Charlie's place?

                  (ELWOOD *stops and listens intently.*)

                  Is Dr Chumley anywhere there? He was
                  there with Mr Dowd earlier in the evening.
                  What? Well, you needn't bite my head off!
                  (*Hangs up.*) My, that man was mad! He said
                  Mr Dowd was welcome any time – but his
                  friend was not!

ELWOOD   That's Mac. Mr McNulty, the bartender. He
                  thinks the world of me. Now, let's all go
                  down to his place and have a drink.

WILSON   Wait a minute –

KELLY   Mr Dowd – (*She goes to him, below desk.*)

ELWOOD   Miss Kelly, may I hold your hand?

KELLY   Yes – If you want to.

                  (*He takes it.*)

                  Poor Mrs Chumley is so worried. Something
                  must have happened to the doctor. Won't
                  you please try and remember something –
                  something else that might help us? Please!

ELWOOD   Miss Kelly, I would do anything in the world
                  for you. I would almost be willing to live my
                  life all over again – almost. But I've told it
                  all.

KELLY   You're sure?

ELWOOD   Quite sure. But won't you ask me again? I
             loved that warm tone in your voice when you
             asked me just now.

SANDERSON   So did I.

WILSON   Nuts!

ELWOOD   (*Turning*) I beg your pardon?

WILSON   Nuts!

ELWOOD   Nuts? Oh, very nice with a glass of port. And
             now I must be going. Harvey and I have
             things to do.

KELLY   What is it you do, Mr Dowd?

ELWOOD   (*Leaning over desk towards* L. *reflectingly*) Well –
             we sit in the bars – have a drink or two – and
             play the juke-box. (*Sits chair* R. *of desk.*)

             (KELLY *sits* L. *of desk.* SANDERSON *is standing* C.
             facing ELWOOD, WILSON U.S.R. *between table
             and window, also facing.*)

             Soon the faces of the other people turn
             towards me and they smile. They're saying,
             "We don't know your name, Mister, but
             you're all right." Harvey and I warm
             ourselves in these golden moments. We came
             as strangers – soon we have friends. They
             come over. They sit with us. They drink with
             us. They talk to us. They tell us about the
             great big terrible things they've done, and all
             the great big wonderful things they're going
             to do. Their hopes – their regrets. Their
             loves – their hates. All very large, because
             nobody ever brings anything small into a bar.
             Then I introduce them to Harvey – and he's
             bigger and grander than anything they can
             offer me. When they leave, they leave
             impressed. The same people seldom come
             back. That's envy, my dear. There's a little bit
             of envy in the best of us. Too bad, isn't it?

SANDERSON   Dowd – how did you happen to call him
             "Harvey"?

ELWOOD   (*Proudly*) Harvey is his name.

SANDERSON   Yes, but how do you know that?

ELWOOD   Ah! – now that's a very interesting
             coincidence. One night, several years ago, I
             was walking down Fairfax Street – between
             Eighteenth and Nineteenth – you know that
             block?

SANDERSON   Yes, Mr Dowd.

ELWOOD   I'd just helped Ed Hickey into a taxi. Ed had
             been mixing his drinks – and I felt he needed
             "conveying" ... I started to walk down the
             street when I heard a voice saying, "Good
             evening, Mr Dowd." I turned, and there was
             this great big white rabbit leaning against a
             lamp-post. Well, I thought nothing of that!
             Because, when you've lived in a town as long
             as I lived in this one, you get used to the fact
             that everybody knows your name. So I went
             over to chat with him. He said, "Ed's a little
             spiffed tonight – or might I be mistaken?"
             Well, of course he wasn't mistaken. I think
             the world of Ed – but he was spiffed! Well,
             we went on talking, and finally I said, "You
             have the advantage of me. You know my
             name – but I don't know yours." And right
             back at me he said, "What name do you
             like?" Well, I didn't have to think a minute.
             "Harvey" has always been my favourite
             name; so I said, "Harvey". Now this is the
             most interesting part of the whole thing. He
             said, "What a coincidence – my name
             happens to be – 'Harvey'!"

SANDERSON   (*He turns and walks* U.S. *in despair, then goes to
             above desk and leans forward, speaking over*
             ELWOOD's *shoulder*) Dowd, what was your
             father's name?

ELWOOD	John! John Frederick.
SANDERSON	Dowd, when you were a little boy you had a playmate – someone of whom you were very fond – with whom you spent many happy, carefree hours, didn't you?
ELWOOD	Of course, doctor. Didn't you?
SANDERSON	What was his name?
ELWOOD	Clifford. Clifford MacElhinney. Did you know the MacElhinneys, doctor?
SANDERSON	No, Mr Dowd, I didn't.
ELWOOD	Oh, there were a lot of 'em. And they circulated! Wonderful people!
SANDERSON	Think carefully, Dowd. Wasn't there someone, somewhere, some time, whom you knew by the name of "Harvey"? Didn't you know anyone by that name?
ELWOOD	No. No. Never. (*He seems suddenly old and crushed, then his eyes light up.*) Perhaps – that's why I had such hopes of it.
SANDERSON	(*Crossing to* WILSON) All right, Wilson, we'll take Mr Dowd upstairs.
WILSON	I'm taking him nowhere. You made this your show – now you run it. Letting him sit there and get off all that hogwash! Forgetting all about Dr Chumley! O.K. – it's your show – you run it!
SANDERSON	(*Opening doors* U.C.) Come along, Dowd.

(ELWOOD *makes no reply. He is lost in his own dreams, staring out in front of him.* SANDERSON *comes* D.S. *a little and stretches out his hand to* ELWOOD.)

Come along, Elwood –

ELWOOD   (*Coming to life again*) Oh; oh – very well –
                Lyman. (*Rises, holding his hat.*) But I'm afraid
                I won't be able to stay with you long. I
                promised to take Harvey to the floor show.
                (*Sadly.*) Yes.

                (*He goes to the doorway.*)

SANDERSON   (*Ushering* ELWOOD *out and indicating stairs*)
                Upstairs, Mr Dowd.

                (ELWOOD *slowly exits upstairs, followed by*
                SANDERSON. KELLY *picks up the bunch of dahlias
                and follows them out, closing the doors.* WILSON *is
                alone on the stage. He stands for a moment in
                thought, then crosses to desk, looking at his wrist-
                watch. He sits chair* R. *of desk and leans his chin
                on his hand, waiting patiently. Enter* CHUMLEY
                D.L. *running. He gets almost across to* R. *when*
                WILSON *sees him and jumps up excitedly.*)

WILSON   (*Going towards him*) Dr Chumley! Are you all
                right?

CHUMLEY   (*He leans unsteadily against table*) All right? Of
                course I'm all right. (*Pause.*) I'm being
                followed! Lock the door.

                (WILSON *goes to door* D.L. *and turns the key.*)

WILSON   (*Returning* C.) Who's following you?

CHUMLEY   (*Drawing himself up*) None of your business.

                (CHUMLEY *exits into office,* D.R., *stumbling as he
                goes. He is heard to lock the door after him.*
                WILSON *stands* C. *for a moment, perplexed. He
                looks towards the door* D.L. *Gradually he gives way
                to nervousness, then terror. He retreats slowly* U.S.,
                *then with a cry he dives for the light switch,
                switches off the lights and hurriedly exits* U.C.,
                closing the doors behind him. As WILSON *goes out
                we see the hallway still brightly lit, but the stage is
                very dim, and after he has shut the doors we can
                just dintinguish the shapes of the furniture. The
                key is heard to turn in the lock of the door* D.L.

The door slowly opens, the light from outside falling on the opposite wall R. *The door shuts. The invisible* HARVEY *has come in. There is time while* HARVEY *crosses the stage. The key is heard to turn in the lock of* CHUMLEY'S *office* D.R. *The door swings open, on stage, the light from within falling on the opposite wall* L. *The door shuts.* HARVEY *has gone in —)*

AND THE CURTAIN FALLS
END OF ACT II

ACT THREE

TIME: *A few minutes after the Curtain of Act II.*

SET: *The office at Chumley's Rest. As in Act II, Scene 2.*

AT RISE: *The Stage is empty. All doors are closed. The light is very dim, as at the end of the preceding scene.*

The door of CHUMLEY'S *office* D.R. *is flung open, the light from the office striking across the stage and illuminating the figure of* CHUMLEY. *He has staggered in through the door and is standing just on-stage of the door facing off. His face is the picture of terror. His voice is low, frightened and gutteral. He gestures with his hands for the rabbit to leave.*

CHUMLEY	Go away! Go away! (*Drawing himself up.*) You're not there – not there! My name is William R. Chumley and I'm not afraid to die. Oooh! (*With a cry, he slams the door and leans against it. He staggers to the table, leaning on it for support.*) Wilson! Wilson! Wilson!
	(WILSON *runs on* U.C. *and switches on lights. The stage is now bright, as in the beginning of the preceding scene.*)
WILSON	Yes, doctor.
CHUMLEY	Wilson – don't leave me!
WILSON	No, doctor.
CHUMLEY	Get that man Dowd out of here!
WILSON	Yes, doctor. (*Starts to exit* C.)
CHUMLEY	Don't leave me!
WILSON	(*Turning back, confused*) But you said, doctor –
CHUMLEY	Dunphy – on the telephone.
WILSON	Yes, doctor. (*Crossing to desk, switches on dictaphone.*) Dunphy!
FEMALE VOICE	Yes, Wilson?

WILSON	Give that guy Dowd his clothes and get him down here right away.
FEMALE VOICE	O.K., Wilson.
	(WILSON *switches off. There is loud knocking on door* D.L.)
CHUMLEY	Don't leave me!
WILSON	Just a minute, doctor! (*Crosses* D.L. *and opens door*.) Judge Gaffney!
	(*Enter* JUDGE, *followed by* MYRTLE.)
JUDGE	(*Entering*) I want to see Dr Chumley. (*Seeing* CHUMLEY.) Chumley, we've got to talk to you. (*Crossing to* R.C.) This thing is serious.
MYRTLE	(*Just behind* JUDGE) It certainly is.
JUDGE	More serious than you suspect. Where can we go and talk? (*Moves towards* CHUMLEY's *office*.)
CHUMLEY	(*Blocking door*) No, no!
WILSON	He don't want you in his office.
JUDGE	(*Indicating chairs beside table*) Then sit down, Dr Chumley, sit down, Myrtle Mae. (*Puts hat on desk and produces notebook*.)
CHUMLEY	(*Dazed, to* MYRTLE) Sit down, Dr Chumley. (*Pointing to himself*.) Sit down, Myrtle Mae. (*Realises*.) Oh!
	(CHUMLEY *sits* R. *of table*, MYRTLE L. *of table*.)
WILSON	(*Crossing to above table*) Are you O.K., doctor?
CHUMLEY	Don't leave me, Wilson. Don't go.
JUDGE	(*At* C.) Now, Chumley, here are my notes. The facts. (*Looking round cautiously*.) Can anybody hear me?
WILSON	(*Growling*) We can all hear you!

JUDGE	(*Gives* WILSON *a look*) Now, Chumley, has it ever occured to you that there might *be* something like this great white rabbit, Harvey?
MYRTLE	Of course there isn't. And anybody who thinks so is crazy!
CHUMLEY	(*Nervously*) Ha-ha! (*Recovers himself and looks at her.*)
MYRTLE	Well, don't look at me like that. There's nothing funny about me. I'm like my father's family – er – they're all dead.
JUDGE	Now then – my client, Mrs Veta Louise Simmons, under oath swears – that on the morning of November the second, while standing in the kitchen of her home, hearing her name called, turned and saw – this great white rabbit, Harvey. He was staring at her. Resenting the intrusion, she made certain remarks and drove him from the house. He went.
CHUMLEY	What did she say?
JUDGE	She was emphatic. The remarks are not important.
CHUMLEY	I want to know how she got this creature out of her sanatorium...I mean...her home.
MYRTLE	I hate you telling him, Judge. It's not a bit like mother.
WILSON	Go on – what did she say?
JUDGE	Looking him right in the eye, she exclaimed in the heat of anger, "To hell with you!"
CHUMLEY	So. (*Looks round at door* D.R.) To hell with you! (*To* JUDGE.) He left?
JUDGE	Yes, he left. But that's beside the point. (*Crosses to above table.*) The point is –

(SANDERSON *appears in the hallway* U.C. *He looks
through the window in hall, then turns to see*
KELLY *coming down the stairs.*)

–is this perjury, or is it something we can
cope with? I ask for your opinion.

SANDERSON   (*Meeting* KELLY *in doorway* C.) Ruth, there you
are! I've been looking all over for you.

CHUMLEY   (*Rising*) Dr Sanderson!

SANDERSON   (*Turning*) Dr Chumley – You're back!

CHUMLEY   Dr Sanderson, disregard what I said this
afternoon. You are a very astute man and I
want you on my staff.

KELLY   Oh, Lyman! Did you hear?

SANDERSON   Thank you, doctor. (*To* KELLY.) Ruth!

            (KELLY *kisses him and runs off* U.C. *upstairs.*)

MYRTLE   You've just got to keep Uncle Elwood out
here, doctor.

CHUMLEY   No! I want this sanatorium the way it
was – before that man came out here this
afternoon.

MYRTLE   I know what you mean.

CHUMLEY   You do?

MYRTLE   Well, it certainly gets on anyone's nerves the
way Uncle Elwood knows what's going to
happen before it happens. This morning, for
instance, he told us that Harvey told him that
Mrs MacElhinney's Aunt Rose – she lives
next door – would drop in on her
unexpectedly tonight from Cleveland.

CHUMLEY   And did she?

MYRTLE   Did she what?

CHUMLEY   (*Still standing and leaning on the table, looking at*
           MYRTLE) Aunt Rose – did she come – just as
           Harvey said she would?

MYRTLE   Oh yes – these things always turn out the
           way Uncle Elwood says they will. But what of
           it? What do we care about the MacElhinneys?

CHUMLEY   (*Turning away from* MYRTLE *towards door* D.R.)
           Fly specks. I've been living my life among fly
           specks – while round the corner miracles
           have been leaning against lamp-posts!

           (VETA *enters* D.L. *Looks round cautiously.*)

VETA   (*With relief*) Nobody here but people. Good!

MYRTLE   Mother! (*Rises and crosses* C.)

VETA   Now, Myrtle, I've brought Elwood's bedroom
           slippers. (*Showing them.*) Well – why are you
           all just sitting here? I thought you'd be
           signing papers about him.

JUDGE   Sit down, girl. (*Indicates chair* MYRTLE *has*
           vacated.)

           (WILSON *steps forward to offer chair.* VETA *sees*
           him.)

VETA   Oh no. Not there. You come over here,
           Myrtle. (*Pulls* MYRTLE *to* L.C. *and sits chair* R.
           of desk.) Well – is everything settled?

           (JUDGE *sits chair* L. *of desk.* MYRTLE *stands above*
           desk.)

CHUMLEY   It soon will be.

SANDERSON (*Crossing to* R. *above table*) Doctor, may I give
           my opinion?

VETA   *Your* opinion? H'm! (*To* JUDGE.) Omar, he's
           the doctor I told you about. The eyes.

SANDERSON It's my opinion that Elwood P Dowd is
           suffering from third-degree hallucination,
           and the (*pointing to* VETA's *back*) other party

concerned is the victim of auto-suggestion. I
recommend shock formula 977 for him, and
bed-rest at home for – (*Points again.*)

CHUMLEY   You do?

SANDERSON   That's my diagnosis, doctor. (*Going towards*
VETA.) You brother won't see this rabbit any
more after we've given him this injection.
We've used it on hundreds on psychopathic
cases.

VETA   Don't you call my brother a psychopathic
case. There's never been anything like that in
our family.

MYRTLE   If you didn't think Uncle Elwood was
psychopatic – why did you bring him out
here?

VETA   Well, where else could I take him? I couldn't
take him to jail, could I? Besides, this is not
your uncle's fault. Why did Harvey have to
speak to him in the first place? With the town
full of people, why did he have to bother
Elwood?

JUDGE   Stop putting your oar in. (*Leaning towards her*
over desk, slightly rising from his chair.) Keep
you oar – out! If this shock formula brings
people back to reality – give it him. That's
where we want Elwood.

CHUMLEY   But I doubt if it would work in a case of this
kind.

SANDERSON   It always has.

VETA   Harvey always follows him home.

CHUMLEY   He does?

VETA   Yes. But if you give Elwood the formula and
he doesn't see Harvey, he won't let him in.
Then when Harvey comes to the door, I'll
deal with him!

MYRTLE   (*Moving down to* R. *of* VETA) Mother, will you
            please stop talking about Harvey as if there
            was such a thing?

VETA   Myrtle Mae Simmons! You've got a lot to
            learn – and I hope you never learn it!

            (ELWOOD *is heard off, humming.*)

JUDGE   Sh! Here he is.

ELWOOD   (*Enters* U.C.) Oh – good evening, everybody!

VETA   Good evening, Elwood. (*Rising and taking
            slippers.*) I've brought you your bedroom
            slippers.

ELWOOD   Oh, thank you, Veta.

            (VETA *gives it up and returns to chair. There is
            an embarrassed silence.*)

JUDGE   Well, what are we going to do, doctor? We've
            got to do something.

VETA   Oh yes – we must.

MYRTLE   I should say so.

CHUMLEY   (*Looking at door* D.R.) Yes, it's imperative.

ELWOOD   Well, while we're all making up our minds
            let's go over to Charlie's place and have a
            drink.

VETA   You're not going anywhere, Elwood. You're
            staying here.

MYRTLE   Yes, Uncle Elwood.

JUDGE   Stay here, boy.

ELWOOD   I intend to leave – you want me to stay. An
            element of conflict is a good thing in any
            discussion. It means everyone is taking part
            and no one is left out. I like that. (*Crosses
            towards* CHUMLEY.) Oh, doctor how did you
            get on with Harvey?

CHUMLEY   Sh!

JUDGE	We're waiting for your answer, doctor!
CHUMLEY	What's that?
JUDGE	What is your decision?
CHUMLEY	I must be alone with this man. If you'll all go into the other room, I'll give you my diagnosis in a moment.
VETA	(*Rising*) Do hurry, doctor.
CHUMLEY	I will.
	(SANDERSON *crosses and opens door* U.L. MYRTLE *exits, followed by* SANDERSON *and* JUDGE. WILSON *exits* U.C., *closing the doors behind him.* VETA *follows the* JUDGE, *with* ELWOOD *close behind her.*)
ELWOOD	We'll all go into the other room.
VETA	(*Turning and pushing him back*) Oh no. Not you, Elwood. You're staying here. (*She exits, closing door.*)
	(CHUMLEY *and* ELWOOD *are left alone.* CHUMLEY *by table* R., ELWOOD *above desk.*)
CHUMLEY	Mr Dowd, let me give you a chair! (*Indicates chair* L. *of table.*)
ELWOOD	(*Crossing to chair*) Thank you, doctor.
CHUMLEY	(*Taking box of cigars from bookcase* R.) Let me give you – a cigar!
ELWOOD	(*Taking cigar*) Oh, thank you very much, doctor. (*Sits.*)
CHUMLEY	Mr Dowd – (*Leaning to him across table.*) What kind of a man are you? Where do you come from?
ELWOOD	Didn't I give you one of my cards?
CHUMLEY	Where – on the face of this tired old earth – did you ever find a thing like him?
ELWOOD	Harvey, the pooka?

CHUMLEY	(*Sits chair* R. *of table*) Now, is it true that he has a function? That he –
ELWOOD	That he gets advance notice? Certainly it's true. Harvey is versatile. Harvey can stop clocks. You've heard the expression, "His face would stop a clock"?
CHUMLEY	Yes. But why? To what purpose?
ELWOOD	Harvey says that he can look at your clock and stop it. And you can go away as long as you like and as far as you like – and with whoever you like – and when you come back – not one minute has ticked by.
CHUMLEY	You mean that he actually...
ELWOOD	Einstein has overcome time and space. Harvey has not only overcome time and space – but – any objections!
CHUMLEY	And does he do this for you?
ELWOOD	Well, he's perfectly willing to – but up to the present I've never known anywhere I'd rather be. You see, I always have a wonderful time wherever I am. I'm having a good time now, doctor.
CHUMLEY	I know where I'd go.
ELWOOD	Where?
CHUMLEY	I'd go to Pittsburgh.
ELWOOD	Pittsburgh?
CHUMLEY	There's a roadhouse outside Pittsburgh, in a grove of maple trees. Cool – green – beautiful.
ELWOOD	My favourite tree!
CHUMLEY	I'd go there with a beautiful young woman. A strange woman. A quiet woman.
ELWOOD	Under a tree?

CHUMLEY   I wouldn't even want to know her name. I'd
           be just – Mr Brown.

ELWOOD   Why wouldn't you want to know her name?
           You might have mutual friends.

CHUMLEY   I wouldn't want any friends.

ELWOOD   Not under that tree.

CHUMLEY   I would send out for some cold beer. I'd talk
           to her. I'd tell her things – things that I've
           never told anyone. Things that are locked in
           here. (*Beats his breast.*)

           (ELWOOD *looks over at his chest with interest.*)

           And then – I'd send for some more cold
           beer.

ELWOOD   No whisky?

CHUMLEY   Beer is best!

ELWOOD   Maybe – under a tree. But the lady might
           like a cocktail.

CHUMLEY   I wouldn't let her talk to me – but as I talked
           I'd want her to stretch out a soft, cool hand
           and stroke my head and say, "Poor thing!
           Oh, you poor, poor thing!"

           (CHUMLEY *puts out his hand and rests it on*
           ELWOOD's, *which is on the table.* ELWOOD *slowly
           draws his hand away, looking rather frightened at*
           CHUMLEY.)

ELWOOD   How long would you want this to go on?

CHUMLEY   Three weeks.

ELWOOD   Cold beer, Pittsburgh and "Poor, poor thing"
           for three weeks? Wouldn't that get a trifle
           monotonous?

CHUMLEY   No, no, it would not. It would be wonderful!

ELWOOD   Well, I think you're making a great mistake
              in not allowing that woman to talk. If she
              gets around at all she might have some very
              interesting little news items. And I'm sure
              you're making a mistake with all that cold
              beer and no whisky. But it's your three
              weeks.

CHUMLEY   (*Dreamily*) Cold beer! Pittsburgh! And one last
              fling! (*Drawing up his legs in ecstasy.*) Oh, my
              God!

ELWOOD   (*Shaken*) Is there anything I could get for
              you, doctor?

CHUMLEY   What – did you have in mind?

ELWOOD   (*Getting up agitatedly*) Now, doctor, I really
              must be going. (*Makes for door* U.L.)

CHUMLEY   (*Rising quickly and moving* L.C. *to stop him*) No,
              no, Mr Dowd. Not in there.

ELWOOD   But I can't leave without saying good night to
              my friend Dr Sanderson.

CHUMLEY   Dr Sanderson is not your friend. None of
              these people are your friends. (*Coming slowly*
              R. *towards him.*) I want you to know that I –
              and I alone – am your friend.

ELWOOD   (*Retreating nervously to table*) Thank you,
              doctor. I'm your friend, too.

CHUMLEY   And this sister of yours – she's at the bottom
              of this conspiracy against you. She's tried to
              persuade me to lock you up. She had your
              commitment papers drawn up. She's got your
              power of attorney. She's got the key to your
              safety-box. She brought you out here this
              afternoon –

ELWOOD   And Veta did all that in one afternoon? My,
              she certainly is a whirlwind!

CHUMLEY   (*Breaking* L. *below desk*) Good God, man,
              haven't you any righteous indignation?

ELWOOD   (*Going to him*) Doctor, when I was a little boy,
              my mother used to say to me, "Elwood" – she
              always called me "Elwood" – "as you go
              through life you must be either 'oh, so
              smart,' or 'oh, so pleasant.' " For years – I
              was smart. I recommend pleasant. You may
              quote me.

CHUMLEY   Just the same, I'm going to protect you even
              if I have to commit her. Would you like me
              to do that?

ELWOOD   Of course not, doctor. Oh, not that you don't
              have a very pleasant place out here. But I'm
              sure Veta would be happier at home with me
              and Harvey and Myrtle Mae.

              (KELLY *enters from* U.C., *carrying some
              magazines. She has removed her nurse's cap and
              wears one of the dahlias in her hair. She goes to
              put magazines on table.*)

              (*Seeing* KELLY *and turning to her.*) Miss Kelly,
              "Diviner grace has never brightened this
              enchanting face." (*To* CHUMLEY.) Ovid's fifth
              Elegy. (*To* KELLY.) My dear, you will never
              look lovelier.

KELLY   (*Crossing to him*) I shall never feel happier,
              Mr Dowd, I know it. (*She kisses* ELWOOD *on the
              cheek, then sees* CHUMLEY *looking at her. Her
              smile fades.*) Yes, doctor! (*She exits* U.C.)

ELWOOD   I wish I knew a little more of that poem!

CHUMLEY   Mr Dowd, do women often come up to you
              and kiss you – as Miss Kelly did just now?

ELWOOD   Every once in a while. And, doctor – I
              encourage it!

CHUMLEY   (*Crossing* D.S. *to* R.) I'm going to keep that
              rabbit for myself.

ELWOOD   What did you say, doctor?

CHUMLEY	Oh, nothing. Nothing. Go ahead and knock if you want to.
	(ELWOOD *starts for the door* U.L. *just as* SANDERSON *comes out.*)
ELWOOD	Dr Sanderson, I couldn't leave without...
SANDERSON	Just a minute, Dowd. (*Crosses to* CHUMLEY *at* D.S.R.) Doctor, do you agree with my diagnoses?
CHUMLEY	Yes. Yes, call them all in.
SANDERSON	Thank you, doctor. (*Back to* C., *calling off.*) Mrs Simmons – Judge Gaffney – will you step in here for a minute, please?
VETA	(*Entering, to* C.) Is everything settled?
	(JUDGE *and* MYRTLE *enter, to* L.C.)
CHUMLEY	(*At* D.R.) I find I concur with Dr Sanderson.
MYRTLE	Oh, that's wonderful! What a relief!
JUDGE	Good boy!
VETA	Isn't that nice?
ELWOOD	Well, let's celebrate. (*Crosses to desk, takes little book out of pocket and sits chair* R. *of desk.*) I've got some new bars listed in this book. We'll look one up and go to it.
SANDERSON	(*Speaking to others in low tone*) Mrs Simmons – Judge Gaffney.
	(*They cross to him with* MYRTLE *as well.*)
	This shock-formula carries a very violent reaction. We cannot give it to him without his consent. Now, will he give it?
VETA	Of course he will, if I ask him.
MYRTLE	Don't ask him. Just give it him.
CHUMLEY	Yes, give it to him.

ELWOOD	Now, there's Casey's Tavern, Dinty Moore's, Hoppy's Hop Inn...how many of us will there be, Veta?
VETA	(*Starts to count*) Well, there's one, two, three...(*Stops.*) Oh, Elwood!
CHUMLEY	(*Solemnly*) Mr Dowd, I have a formula – 977 – that will be good for you. Will you take it?
JUDGE	You won't see this rabbit any more.
SANDERSON	But you will see your responsibilities – your duties –
ELWOOD	(*Rises and crosses to* CHUMLEY) Well, doctor, if you thought of it, it must be pretty good. And if I run into anyone I think needs it – I'll recommend it. As for myself, I wouldn't care for it.
	(*They are all in despair.*)
VETA	You hear that, Judge. You hear that, doctor. That's what we have to put up with.
ELWOOD	(*Turning to her*) But, Veta – do *you* want me to take this?
VETA	(*Coming* D.S. *to* L. *of* ELWOOD) Oh, Elwood, I'm only thinking of you. You're my brother, and I've known you for years! I'd do anything for you. That Harvey wouldn't do anything for you. He's making a fool of you, Elwood. Don't be made a fool of.
ELWOOD	Oh, I won't!
VETA	Why, you could amount to something! You could be sitting on the Western Slope Water Board right now if only you'd ask them.
ELWOOD	Well, if that's what you want, Harvey and I will go over and ask them tomorrow.
VETA	I never want to see another tomorrow – not if Myrtle and I have to live in the house with that rabbit. Our friends never come to see us;

	we have no social life – we have no life at all. We're both miserable. Oh, I wish I could die – but maybe you don't care! (*She moves to chair* R. *of desk and sits there crying.*)
ELWOOD	Veta! Veta – my dear! (*Going to her.*) I've always wanted Veta to have everything she needs. I've only wanted her to be happy. (*To* VETA.) Veta, are you sure?
	(*She nods.*)
	(*Going to* CHUMLEY, *very seriously.*) All right, doctor. I'll take it. Where do I go?
CHUMLEY	In Dr Sanderson's office, Dowd.
ELWOOD	(*Moves towards door* U.L., *stops and turns*) Well – you'll say good-bye to the old fellow for me, won't you? (*He exits* U.L.)
SANDERSON	(*Following him out*) I'll see to all the preparations, doctor.
JUDGE	How long will this take, doctor?
CHUMLEY	Not long. Only a few minutes. Why don't you wait? (*He exits* U.C.).
	(VETA *is still sitting in chair* R. *of desk.* MYRTLE *goes to window* R. *and starts examining the curtains.* JUDGE *moves to door* U.L. *and bends down, looking through keyhole.*)
VETA	Dr Chumley said it wouldn't take long.
MYRTLE	Now, mother, don't fidget. (*Holding curtain.*) Isn't this stunning material? (*Drapes curtain round her.*) Mother, could you see me in a house-coat of this material?
VETA	Dr Chumley said...(*To* MYRTLE.) Yes, dear – but let me get a good night's sleep first. (*She crosses* R., *puts her bag on table and sits chair* L. *of table.*)
	(*There is a loud knocking at the door* D.L. JUDGE *springs up and jumps into chair* L. *of desk.*)

JUDGE	Come in!
	(*Enter a* CAB DRIVER.)
	What do you want?
CABBY	I'm looking for a lady in a light-coloured...(*Sees* VETA.) Oh, there you are! (*Crossing to her.*) Lady – you jumped out of my cab without paying me.
VETA	Oh yes. I forgot. How much?
CABBY	All the way out here from town? Three dollars.
VETA	(*Looking in bag*) Well, I could have sworn I brought my purse with me. Where is it? (*Turns out bag. There is no purse.*) Well, of all things – Myrtle, have you got any money?
MYRTLE	No, I spent that money Uncle Elwood gave me on my new hair-do for the party. (*She turns away, picks up book from bookcase and starts looking idly through it.*)
VETA	Judge, have you got three dollars I could give this man?
JUDGE	Sorry! I've got a cheque.
CABBY	We don't take cheques.
	(CHUMLEY *enters* U.C. *He has his white jacket on and is carrying a hypodermic syringe and a phial of 977.*)
VETA	Dr Chumley, could you lend me three dollars to pay this taxi-driver?
CHUMLEY	Well – I haven't my wallet on me. No time to get it now. He's in there having an injection. Sorry. (*Exits* U.L.)
VETA	Well, I'll have to get it from my brother. But I can't get it right now. He's in there having an injection. It won't be long. You'll have to wait.

CABBY	You're goin' to get my money from your brother, and he's in there getting some of that stuff they shoot into 'em out here?
VETA	Yes. It'll only be a few minutes.
CABBY	Lady – I want my money now!
VETA	But I told you it'll only be a few minutes. Besides, I want you to drive us back to town, anyway.
CABBY	And I told *you* – I want my money now! – or I'm nosin' the cab back to town, and you can wait for the bus! – at six in the morning!
VETA	Well, of all the pig-headed, stubborn things!
MYRTLE	I should say so!
JUDGE	What's the matter with you?
CABBY	Nothin' that three dollars won't fix. You 'eard me – take it or leave it!
VETA	(*Crossing to door,* U.L.) Well, I never heard of anything so unreasonable in my life! (*Knocks.*) Dr Chumley – will you let Elwood out for a minute!
CHUMLEY	(*Off*) Well, it's very inconvenient – but if you insist.
	(*Opens door and* ELWOOD *enters putting on jacket.*)
	(*Following him on.*) Only be a minute, Mr Dowd.
VETA	Elwood, I came out without my purse. Will you give this man three dollars. But don't give him any more. He's been very rude.
ELWOOD	(*Crossing to* CABBY *at* R.C.) Good evening. Dowd's the name – Elwood P.
CABBY	Mine's Lofgren – E. J.

ELWOOD	Glad to meet you, Mr Lofgren. This is my sister, Mrs Simmons – my charming little niece, Miss Myrtle Mae Simmons, Judge Gaffney and Dr Chumley. (*Indicating them in turn.*)
	(*There is a pause.*)
	Have – er – have you lived around these parts long, Mr Lofgren?
CABBY	All my life.
ELWOOD	And are you happy in your work?
CABBY	Oh – it's O.K. I've been with Apex Cabs for fifteen years now, and my brother Joe's been driving for Brown Cabs – pretty nearly twelve.
ELWOOD	You drive for Apex and your brother Joe for Brown. Well, now, isn't that interesting, Veta?
CHUMLEY	(*Coughing*) Better get on with this, Mr Dowd.
ELWOOD	Certainly. (*To* CABBY.) Now, let me give you one of my cards. My sister and my charming little niece live with me at that address. You must come and have dinner with us some time.
CABBY	Sure. Be glad to.
ELWOOD	When – would you be glad to?
CABBY	Well, I couldn't come any night but Tuesday. I'm on duty all the rest of the week.
ELWOOD	Then you must come on Tuesday. We'll expect you and be delighted to see you. Won't we, Veta?
VETA	(*Disgusted*) Oh, Elwood, I'm sure this man has friends of his own!
ELWOOD	(*Reproachfully*) My dear! One can't have too many friends.

(CHUMLEY *coughs.*)

VETA   Elwood, don't keep Dr Chumley waiting.
                That's rude. (*She goes to* U.S.C. *and waits,
                resting a hand on chair.*)

ELWOOD   Of course! (*Handing* CABBY *a note.*) Now,
                there's five dollars – keep the change. I'm
                glad to have met you, and we'll expect you
                on Tuesday with your brother. You must
                excuse me now. Good night – my dear
                fellow! (*Exits* U.L. *As he passes* JUDGE, *sitting at
                desk.*) A dear fellow, Judge!

                (CHUMLEY *follows him off and closes door.*)

CABBY   What a lovely man!

VETA   (*Coming* D.S. *and sitting chair* L. *of table*)
                Certainly – but you could just as well have
                waited.

CABBY   (*At* L.C.) Oh no. listen, lady. I've been driving
                this route for fifteen years. I've brought 'em
                out here to get that stuff, and I've drove 'em
                back after they've had it. It changes 'em!

VETA   Well, I certainly hope so!

CABBY   And you ain't kiddin'? On the way out here
                they sit back and enjoy the ride. They talk to
                me. Sometimes we stop and watch the sunsets
                – and look at the birds flying. Sometimes we
                stop and watch birds when there ain't no
                birds, and look at the sunsets when it's
                raining. We have a swell time, and I always
                get a big tip. But afterwards –oh, oh! (*Turns
                and makes for door* D.L.)

VETA   Afterwards, oh, oh? What do you mean –
                afterwards, oh, oh?

CABBY   Oh – they nag, nag, nag! They yell at me.
                "Watch the brakes, watch the lights, watch
                the crossings!" they scream at me to hurry.
                They've got no faith – in me or me cab! But

	it's the same cab! – the same driver! And we're goin' back over the very same road! It's no fun – and no tips! (*Makes for door again.*)
VETA	Oh, but my brother would have tipped you, anyway. He's very generous. Always has been.
CABBY	Not after this he won't be! Lady – after this he'll be a perfectly normal 'uman being – and you know what bastards they are! (*Exits* D.L.)
VETA	(*Rises and rushes to door* U.L., *banging on it*) Stop it! Stop it! Don't give it to him! Elwood, come out of there!
	(JUDGE *and* MYRTLE *rush to her and pull her away.*)
MYRTLE	Mother – stop it!
JUDGE	Dr Chumley is giving the injection.
	(*They drag her* D.S.R., *protesting.*)
VETA	(*Quite hysterical*) But I don't want him to have it! I don't want Elwood that way! I don't like people like that!
MYRTLE	Mother, stop it! Do something to her, Judge!
VETA	(*Rounding on* MYRTLE) You be quiet! I've lived longer than you have! I remember my father!
CHUMLEY	(*Enters* U.L.) What's all this?
	(WILSON *runs on from* C.)
JUDGE	She wants to stop the injection!
VETA	(*Crossing to him*) Doctor, you haven't already given it to him, have you?
CHUMLEY	No, but we're ready. Wilson! – get Mrs Simmons out of here!
	(WILSON *goes to seize her.*)

VETA	Leave me alone! Take your hands off me, you white slaver!
JUDGE	You don't know what you want. You didn't want that rabbit either.
VETA	(*Coming* D.S.C.) And what's wrong with Harvey? If Elwood and Myrtle Mae and I want to live with Harvey that's nothing to do with you! You don't even have to come around. It's our business.

(ELWOOD *enters* U.L. VETA *runs to him.*)

Elwood! Elwood!

(*She buries her face against him.*)

ELWOOD	There, there. Veta's all tired out. She's done a lot today.
JUDGE	(*Crossing and taking hat from desk*) Well, have it your own way. I'm not going to give up my game at the club – I don't care how big the animal is! (*Exits* D.L.)
MYRTLE	Me too. (*Crossing after* JUDGE.) I'll wait for you in the cab, mother. (*Exits* D.L.)
VETA	Oh yes – the cab. (*Crossing to table* R.) Come on, Elwood, let's get out of here. I hate this place – I wish I'd never seen it!
CHUMLEY	But – Mrs Simmons – I insist!
ELWOOD	It's whatever Veta says, doctor.
VETA	(*Looking in bag*) Why, look at this! (*Holds up purse.*) My purse! Well, I know it wasn't there five minutes ago – or I could have paid that taxi-man myself. (*A smile spreads over her face as she whispers, almost to herself.*) Harvey! Oh, well – come along, Elwood – hurry up! (*She exits* D.L.)
ELWOOD	(*At* C., *to* CHUMLEY, *who has come* D.S.R.) Well – good night, doctor.

CHUMLEY	(*Quietly pleased*) Good night, Mr Dowd.
ELWOOD	(*Going to* WILSON, *at* U.S.R.) Good night, Mr Wilson. Ha-ha! You're crazy all right!
VETA	(*Off*) Come along, Elwood!
ELWOOD	(*Going towards door* D.L.) Coming! (*Turning back to* L.C.) You know, doctor, I've always known what my family think of Harvey. I've often wondered what Harvey's family think about me.

(*The door* D.R. *opens.*)

Oh, there you are! Doctor – please! You're standing in his way!

(CHUMLEY *backs* U.S. *a little to let* HARVEY *pass in front of him. The invisible* HARVEY *crosses to* ELWOOD.)

I've been looking all over for you. Now, where've you been? You haven't! Come on, now – we're late for Charlie's place!

(ELWOOD *links arms with* HARVEY *and they cross to door* D.L. CHUMLEY *stands with arms outstretched towards* HARVEY, WILSON *is staring from* U.R.)

As ELWOOD *and* HARVEY *exit* –

THE CURTAIN FALLS

END OF PLAY

PROPERTY PLOT

Act I, Scene 1

ON STAGE
Furniture, etc.
   Red tapestry chair, D.S. of fireplace, L.
   Mantelpiece attached to flat, L.
   Fireplace inset in flat, L.
   Bookcase inset in flat, U.L.
   Oval black table in front of bookcase, U.L.
   Black rug, 6 ft. × 4 ft., in front of fireplace, L.
   Red tapestry chair, L. of window, U.C.
   Carpet, 16 ft. × 10 ft., covering R. and C. of stage.
   Heavy green pelmet and curtains, back flat, A.
   Round table, 3 ft. diameter, D.R.
   2 upholstered armchairs, L. and R. of round table.
   Dummy painted bookcase in flat, back R.
   Cream tapestry armchair, R. of oval table.

Small Properties
   Mantelpiece, D.L.
      2 brass horse ornaments, one at either end.
      2 small vases, U.S. and D.S. of horses.
      1 black wooden fan, C., leaning against flat.

   Over mantelpiece:
      Oil-painting of the late Marcella Pinney Dowd, Veta's mother.

   Fireplace:
      Fire screen.
      Brass fender.
      Pots of ferns inside fender.

   Bookcase, U.L.:
      Sets of leather-bound volumes.
      Copy of "Pride and Prejudice," by Jane Austen, C.

   Oval table in front of bookcase:
      Telephone, front R.
      Small vase of violets, back C.
      2 vases of red roses, back L. and R.
      Silver tray, front C., with 4 glasses, decanter of whisky and siphon.
      China ash-tray, L. of tray.

   Door, U.L.C.:
      Key on inside of door.
      Non-practical double light-switch, D.S. of door-frame.

   Flat U.C. to L. of window:
      2 oil-paintings in gilt frames, one above the other.

PROPERTY PLOT—*continued*

Round table, R.:
    Vase of mixed roses.
    China ash-tray.

Armchair L. of round table:
    2 loose red cushions.

Backing, R.:
    2 antique pictures.

Electric fittings
    2 wall-brackets, practical, one each side of fireplace.
    4 shades for above.

OFF STAGE
    U.L. Harvey's overcoat.
         Harvey's hat, with two holes in crown.
    D.R. Speaker for panatrope-effect, "Pale bands I love," at curtain-rise.
         Tea-cups for noises of party.

ACT I, SCENE 2

ON STAGE
Furniture, etc.
    Large office desk, L.C.
    Small square gate-leg table, R.C.
    Combined bookcase and filing cabinet, U.R. Filing-cabinet portion is at D.S.
        end.
    Long striped curtains and pelmet and pair net curtains, window-flat, U.R.C.
    Net curtain to window in backing, U.L.C.
    Pedestal ash-tray between doors, L.
    3 chairs: R. of desk, L. of table and against flat between window and double
        doors, U.C.
    2 arm-chairs: L. of desk and R. of table.

Small Properties
    Desk, L.C.:
        Dictaphone, practical, U.S.
        Reading-lamp, non-practical, U.S.
        Press-button for buzzer, practical, U.S.
        Telephone, D.S.
        Large blotting-pad, L.C.
        Inkstand and pen rack with two inkwells, red and black, R.C.
        Glass ash-tray, D.S. of inkstand.
        Telephone directory, American, on top of appointments book, D.S.L.
        Scribbling pad, D.S. of blotting pad.
        White correspondence cards, U.S. of blotting pad.
        2 pencils on inkstand.
        Ebony ruler, L. of inkstand.
        Desk calendar, U.S. of inkstand.
        Blank foolscap form on blotting pad.
    Hall-backing, U.C.:
        1 flower picture in modern frame.

PROPERTY PLOT—*continued*

Stair-backing, U.C.:
    1 brown china light switch and block, non-practical.
Back-flat to L. of double doors, U.C.:
    2 flower pictures in modern frames.
Back-flat to R. of double doors, U.C.:
    Double inset electric light switch, non-practical.
Table, R.C.:
    3 American magazines.
    Veta's handbag.
Bookcase, U.R.:
    Books in shelves.
    Panel at top of U.S. section, fronted by dummy books, with catch allowing
      it to swing open.
    Practical alarm bell, with coloured lights in panel, behind dummy panel
      above.
    On top of combined bookcase and filing cabinet:
        3 brown bowls containing pots of carnations.
        Glass ash-tray.
        Cigar box containing cigars.
    In filing cabinet:
        Various files and papers.
        Printed cards, about 8 in. X 5 in.
    In bottom shelf of bookcase:
        1 set encyclopædias.

Electric Fittings
    3 sets of wall brackets, practical: L. between doors, U.C., and R. above
      bookcase.
    6 shades for above.

Miscellaneous
    Door U.L. Name-plate, DR. LYMAN SANDERSON.
    Door D.R. Name-plate, DR. WILLIAM CHUMLEY.
    Door D.L. Key on inside of door.

OFF STAGE
    U.L.   Harvey's hat and coat.
           Wilson's hat and coat.
           Board with clip and paper and pencil.
    R.   Chumley's hat, coat and gloves.
           Book for Chumley.

ACT II, SCENE 1

ON STAGE
    As Act I, Scene 1, except key out of door, L.C.

OFF STAGE
    L.   Picture of Elwood and Harvey, wrapped in brown paper and tied with
string.
    L.   Wooden box, covered felt, and mallet (for noise effect).

PROPERTY PLOT—*continued*

ACT II, SCENE 2
ON STAGE
As Act I, Scene 2, except:
Curtains drawn.
3 books set D.S. on desk.

OFF STAGE
U.L.   2 piles of books.
        Webbing strap.
D.L.   Bunch of dahlias.
        Large lock and key, for effect.
D.R.   Large lock and key, for effect.
        Rod for operating door. (Rod is pushed along floor. The on-stage end is turned up at right-angles and fits into small saddle at bottom of door.)

ACT III
ON STAGE
As Act II, Scene 2, except:
No books on desk.
Inkstand and ruler moved on to blotting pad.

OFF STAGE
U.L.   Magazines (Kelly).
        Hypodermic syringe and phial of 977 (Chumley).
        Chumley's white coat.
U.L.   Elwood's bedroom-slippers (Veta).
D.R.   Rod for operating door.

PERSONAL PROPERTIES

ELWOOD	Visiting cards.	Act I, Scene 2, and Act III.
	Playing cards.	Act I, Scene 2.
	Cigarette case and one cigarette.	Act I, Scene 2.
	Piece of paper with telephone number.	Act III, Scene 1.
	Five-dollar bills.	Act III.
	Notebook.	Act III.
VETA	Handbag, with compact, purse and handkerchief.	Act I, Scene 2, Act II, Scene 1, and Act III.
CHUMLEY	Spectacles.	Act I, Scene 2, and Act III.
	Notebook.	Act I, Scene 2.
SANDERSON	Spectacles.	Act I, Scene 2.
	Lighter.	Act I, Scene 2.
JUDGE	Notebook and pencil.	Act II, Scene 1, and Act II.
BETTY	Pencil in handbag.	Act I, Scene 2.
KELLY	Dahlia.	Act III.
MYRTLE	Spectacles.	Act I, Scene 1.
		Act II, Scene 1, and Act IIII.

WARDROBE PLOT

ELWOOD

Brown sports-jacket.
Check trousers.
Sports-shirt.
Bow tie.
Brown shoes.
Brown trilby bat, the brim turned up.

VETA

Act I, Scene 1

Dark blue satin long dinner-dress.
2 diamante clips at neck.
Dark blue sandal-shoes.

Act I, Scene 2, Act III
Clover-pink dress and long coat, the coat lined violet.
Belt to match.
Violet felt hat, pink ribbon.
Brown calf and suede shoes.
Violet ninon scarf.
Pale beige gloves.
Brown calf handbag.

Act II, Scene 1
As Act I, Scene 2, but separate violet hat, very tattered, with the ribbon hanging down in pieces.

CHUMLEY

Black coat and vest.
Black striped trousers.
Black Homburg hat.
Black shoes and socks.
White shirt and collar, black tie.
White handkerchief.
Also, for Act I, Scene 2, and Act III:
Starched white hospital jacket, buttoning on shoulder.

SANDERSON

Dark brown double-breasted suit.
Brown shoes.
White shirt and collar, brown tie.
Also, for Act I, Scene 2:
White hospital jacket, as Chumley.

WILSON

White single-breasted jacket.
White vest.
White trousers.
White rubber-soled shoes.
Brown belt for trousers.

WARDROBE PLOT—*continued*

	Also, for Act I, Scene 2, and Act II, Scene 1.:
	Brown overcoat.
	Brown trilby hat.

KELLY   White sharkskin dress and belt.
                 White suede shoes.
                 White nurse's cap.
                 White petticoat.
                 White stockings.

MYRTLE   *Act I, Scene 1*
                 Pink party dress, trimmed sequins.
                 Pink and emerald sash.
                 Pink suede sandals.
                 Act II, Scene 1, and Act III
                 Grey wool two-piece dress.
                 Tan sling-back shoes.
                 Tan material bag *(Act III)*.

GAFFNEY   Dark grey suit, single-breasted, with waistcoat.
                 White shirt and wing-collar.
                 Bow tie.
                 Black shoes.
                 Black Homburg hat, not worn.

CABBY   Peaked cap, rather dilapidated.
                 Raincoat over lounge suit.
                 Scarf.
                 Brown shoes.

BETTY   Black costume, trimmed at waist with sequins.
                 Black hat, trimmed flowers and veiling.
                 Orchids on costume.
                 Black shoes.
                 Fawn suede gloves.
                 Black silk bag.

MRS. CHAUVENET   Mustard-coloured dress.
                 Brown coat, trimmed fur and lined mustard.
                 Brown antelope shoes.
                 Brown suede gloves.
                 Long fur flat stole.
                 Jabot lace.
                 Brown cloth bag to match coat.
                 Brown hat, trimmed feathers.

MAID   Long black dress, high collar.
                 White apron.
                 White cap.
                 White cuffs and collar.
                 White petticoat.
                 Black shoes.
                 Black stockings.

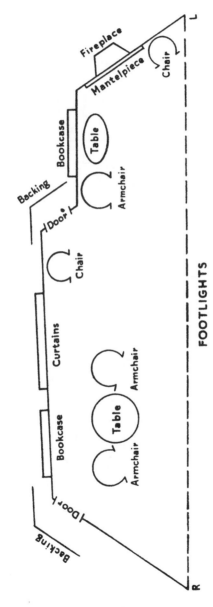

STAGE PLAN for Act I. Sc.I. & Act II. Sc.I.

FOOTLIGHTS

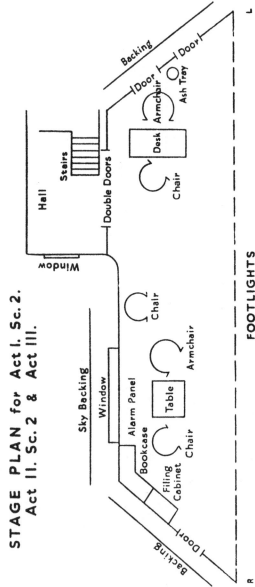

STAGE PLAN for Act I. Sc. 2.
Act II. Sc. 2 & Act III.